Love all -

Raising My Furry Children

Tracy Ahrens

Tracy Ahrens

Guest Story by Steve Dale

Raising My Furry Children

Tracy Ahrens

Guest Story by Steve Dale

Weaving Dreams Publishing
Watseka, Illinois

Weaving Dreams Publishing

Copyright © 2011 by Tracy Ahrens

ISBN # 978-0-9824876-7-9

Library of Congress Control Number
2011923447

www.weavingdreamspublishing.com

Guest Story by Steve Dale

Cover Art by Nancy Burgan
Cover Design by John E. Durkin Designs

Printed in the United States of America
10 9 8 7 6 5 4 3 2

Dedication

To all those who love,
have loved or
will love creatures great and small.

Contents

Introduction

On Dec. 19, 2002, a small cardboard box was found outside of the front door at Kankakee County Animal Control and Adoption Center in Kankakee, Ill.

Taped to the side of the box was a note. Inside were two cats: one was a creamy beige color, while the other was a tabby. Both had long hair, a broad nose, and quarter-sized, golden eyes.

The note read:

"My owner, who is dying, can't take care of us anymore. The beige and white cat's name is Baby. She is one year old and eats dry and canned food twice a day. Her dry food is out all day. For a treat after she eats in the morning, she only likes mozzarella cheese from Aldi's. The other cat is a kitten, and her name is Princess. She eats the same thing and is Baby's baby. She is six months old. Please try to find them a home together – and a good home. They have had no shots and have all their claws. They haven't been spayed either. Sorry to have to do it this way, but there is no other way. I don't have much time left and no money. It has gone to the doctors and for prescriptions. I love my pets, but I cannot take care of them anymore. I can't even take care of myself.

P.S. They get brushed every day, and Princess loves to get vacuumed."

Animal control workers struggled for weeks, even after local newspapers ran stories about the abandoned cats, to find a new owner who would take both cats together.

Sadly, animal control workers in Kankakee, and at shelters across the country, often find similar situations when arriving at work in the morning – animals left in cardboard boxes on the front steps, dogs tied to trees on the property with a bowl of water or a toy beside them and dogs left in outside pens.

People often leave animals anonymously to avoid a small *turn-in* fee.

While it is better for a pet to be deserted at a shelter than on a country road or a city street, little is ever known about the animal's history. This often makes the process of placing them with new owners lengthy and difficult.

Homeless animals cannot speak to explain their health status, how they like to be petted, what they are afraid of, or if they like other cats, dogs and children. Unfortunately, not all shelters are no-kill. That's why working with all possible background information is vital in moving pets quickly to new homes.

Across the country, every year, between six and eight million dogs and cats end up in shelters, looking for new homes (*Humane Society of the United States, July 2008*). Half of these animals are euthanized; the other half finds new homes through adoptions.

Just as many shelters across the country do, Kankakee County Animal Control asks people to share information about their pet when surrendering it. People are given a form on which to write several points of information about their dog or cat, including:

- ✔ How does your cat react to visitors?

- ✔ How and where does the dog like to be petted?

- ✔ Does the dog jump on furniture?

- ✔ How would you describe your cat? Rambunctious, affectionate, vocal, aloof...

- ✔ Is the dog accustomed to: baths, ear cleanings, nail trims, brushing...

And then there is the last question that made me reflect:

- ✔ Is there anything else we should know about this dog/cat?

I thought to myself, my dogs' and cats' personalities and lives could never be summed up on one page of paper. Like people, my pets have biographies waiting to be shared.

Unfortunately, pets can't speak about their likes, dislikes and, sometimes, the abusive lifestyles they have endured. New dog owners sometimes learn that lifting a broom to clean a floor will send their dog running into another room, and that the dog fears beatings it probably received from a previous owner.

Every day with an adopted pet is a learning process. The more you learn, the more you learn to love the new creature you have been blessed with.

If we spend as much time focusing on our pets as

we do with other family members and friends, we'll feel a greater connection, devotion, and love for them. Maybe then, fewer pets will end up in shelters.

Several years ago I began writing down three- to four-word notes to myself. They were notes about funny or touching events that took place in my life between my pets and me. For example,

> Licked the cake
> Destroying the house
> Flatulence.
> Squishy ball
> Hershey bars
> Paper Wads
> Half-a-pack of gum

The stories rushed back to me. Some I shared with friends and family members, and some I haven't had the chance to relive yet. The stories come back to me every day and live in my memory. With each one, I find myself smiling and laughing with pride.

The notes were about my pets, my furry children, my family – my loyal companions every hour I am with them. When I am away from them, they wait for me, looking out of the house windows and occasionally listening to me over the phone with the aid of my answering machine.

My stories started to grow into a larger mental encyclopedia when my now ex-husband and I obtained our Brittany spaniel, Speckles, in 1995. His antics never ceased to amaze us, to make us laugh or to make us frustrated. He used our sofa as a potty training station, he hid bones in our dresser drawers, he blew bubbles in his water dish with his nose and the list went on and on.

My cats, Chocolate Drop (C.D.), Desdemona (Desi), Joan of Arc (Joanie) and Captain Jack Sparrow (Jack) created their own chapters in my encyclopedia of pet tales. Desi once fell into the toilet while in a high-speed chase with Speckles. C.D. catches paper wads like a baseball outfielder. Joan wakes me by sticking her wet nose in my ears. Jack slithers under the backyard fence to patrol surrounding yards.

After Speckles came into my life, I started to find my body and mind calming when I observed his behavior. He is an experiment to me. I sample speaking softly to him, singing to him when he is sleepy, tricking him when we play ball and watching him try to get my attention when I am eating.

When I began observing animal behavior more, I noticed my friends and acquaintances talking about their pets in nearly every conversation. Their stories were similar. Everyone laughed, and I always walked away with a loving feeling inside. This feeling comes from knowing you have connected with an animal, creating a bond between two species that is beyond price.

Pets, I've learned, are like toddlers. We, the parents of these dogs and cats, learn about pet care by sharing our stories. It is an experience similar to learning from fellow mothers and fathers about childcare.

While most people keep health records for their pets, I think it is also important to keep a diary – a book of brief stories that recount your pet's personality.

With time, we often forget certain mishaps and funny situations we share with family, friends, and our pets. Documenting these events allows you to look back years later and laugh about the interactions you had with those you love.

Perhaps, if we all keep a diary of our pet's antics, and that pet has to be placed in a shelter some day, this diary of information can help that pet find a new home faster.

Keeping such documentation may help decrease pet euthanasia rates across the country.

Our nation's love of dogs and cats

As I wrote in my diary about raising my furry children, I also researched facts about pet ownership.

In March of 2008, there were approximately 74.8 million dogs and 88.3 million cats owned by people in the United States (*American Pet Products Manufacturers Association*).

Americans hold surveys to see if dogs or cats rule, they bring dogs to work with them, hold pet beauty pageants, take dogs to special summer camps, and room with pets in hotels while on vacation.

A survey by the American Animal Hospital Association (AAHA) said that eighty percent of pet owners give their dogs holiday or birthday presents, sixty-two percent sign letters or cards from themselves and their dogs, and thirty-three percent talk to their dogs through the phone or answering machine.

Here are more fun facts:

• An April 1999 statistic in *Health* magazine said that eighty-three percent of pet owners said they would risk their life for their pet.
• According to a 1995 survey by the AAHA, forty-

eight percent of female pet owners rely more on their pet than a spouse or child for affection.

• Fifty-eight percent of pet owners love their pet so much that when the pet dies, they will bury it on family property.

Most interesting to me was this – sixty-six percent of the pet owners surveyed agree that their pets are like children to them (*HomeCare Council*).

In a September 2000 *Health* magazine survey, eighty-four percent of pet owners referred to themselves as *pet parents*.

Yes! As I already believed, pets are like children. As they age, they even mature like children. They become our tear wipers, walking partners, dinner guests, and fellow letter readers.

In my research, I also learned that having a close bond with a pet can be beneficial to your health.

Because pets provide laughter, they are furry forms of medication for humans. Laughter, studies have shown, has an amazing healing effect on the body. The effects are similar to exercise: endorphins – natural painkillers – are released, infection-fighting proteins in saliva are released, breathing and circulation increases and much more.

Millions of people in the United States have suppressed immune systems, and thirty to forty percent of these people own companion animals. Pets provide a psychological boost, love and affection, and facilitate interaction for them.

Pets can also help lower blood pressure. Researchers at the State University of New York at Buffalo presented a study in March of 1997 noting that the company of dogs and cats may help lower single women's blood pressure. Research findings were the same for women in their early seventies, as well as for women in their mid-twenties.

The key to all of this, however, is keeping a close bond with your pet.

It doesn't matter what time of day it is, what type of mood I am in, if I am in a hurry or tired after a long day at work, I always acknowledge my pets when I enter a room or when they enter a room.

They look for my attention, and without it, they nudge me with their heads or paws, or speak to me in a gentle voice, whether a grunt, chirping meow or whimper. To me, not acknowledging the presence of a pet or someone else's pet is like ignoring a person who is in a room with you.

I listen to my pets, and watch them when they do not know I am watching them. I anticipate their movements and usually know what they desire of me. They, in turn, have learned to watch me and anticipate my moves, from hitting the snooze button on my alarm clock in the morning, to putting on my coat before leaving for work.

Listening, watching, simply learning from each other is what brings pets and their owners closer together. With these actions comes obedience – pets being obedient to owners and owners being obedient to pets. All this takes time, patience, and respect. Consider writing a pet diary of your own.

The stories you are about to read are narratives of how I learned patience and respect for my pets. They are grouped according to types of animals and not chronological order

Some of the stories have been printed over the years in three different publications: *Pets: Part of the Family* magazine, *Pet Times* newspaper in Chicago and

Russell Publications newspapers based in South Suburban Chicago.

Please, share these stories about raising my furry children.

Enjoy!

Thank you, Chaser

A Guest Story by Steve Dale

In order to tell you about a dog that changed my life, I have to go back fourteen years to the inside of an elevator.

Klop, klunk, kerplunk ... Then we heard an awful-sounding loud clang, and the elevator came to an abrupt halt.

You know how passengers are in an elevator. At first, no one says a word. But, you can tell they are alarmed. They have Barney Fife faces – their eyes speak sheer terror. In this circumstance, they looked to me for action.

So, I took the initiative and sounded the alarm button. Like a dinner bell magnified by a thousand, it rang loud enough to be heard down the block. But no one from our five-story vintage condo building replied.

Finally, one of the passengers spoke up, or should I say, broke up. She melted and began to whimper. Attempting to console her, I touched her shoulder and said, "It's okay. There's no need to worry."

Again, I pushed that yellow alarm button. Then another passenger began to walk in circles.

"Lucy, sit," I said.

Chaser was already positioned in a sit, and the

third passenger, Boots Montgomery, began to bark. She barked even louder when we all heard a voice call-out from the wilderness. The voice was our neighbor Blake saying, "Hello. Is someone in the elevator?"

Over Boots' barking, I explained the problem. Blake called the elevator company and reported back that it might take a rescuer an hour or more to reach the building because he was on the other side of town, and it was rush hour.

My first thought was how lucky I happened to be. After all, we were on our way up rather than down in the elevator. The dogs had already gone outside to do their afternoon business. Our elevator is so antiquated, I swear a rodent going round-and-round in a cylinder that pulls ropes like the elevator in *The Flintstones* operates it.

Poor Lucy was shaking with fright. Lucy, a cute-as-a-button miniature Australian shepherd, was a cocky performer, reveling at showing off her parlor tricks – like playing dead or jumping through a Hula Hoop. She performed her little routines at the Rehabilitation Institute of Chicago and other places as an animal-assisted therapy dog. Like her dad, Lucy is a dog in love with applause. But at this moment, little nineteen-pound Lucy was sounding more like Lucille Ball going "Whaaa!" She was shakier than Jell-O. I held her as she whimpered.

Meanwhile, Boots Montgomery was attempting to climb into my shirt. The poor thing couldn't get any closer to me. Still, true to her nature, every once in a while, she'd bark at an imaginary elevator intruder. Boots Montgomery, a twenty-pound Tibetan terrier, has this philosophy of life: bark first and ask questions later.

I was so busy consoling Lucy and Boots, I barely noticed how unruffled our thirty-five-pound Brittany spaniel, Chaser, was.

Chaser stared at me with her amber eyes. I then realized that she had been looking at me for the entire time we had been trapped – never taking her eyes from me. Now, finally, Chaser had my full attention.

I hugged Chaser and thought about her first days in our home. She was nearly a year old at the time we acquired her through what was presumably a rescue operation. We had no knowledge of her checkered past.

All Chaser did for the first few weeks she spent in our home was urinate and cry. She piddled when I piddled, mostly because I had the audacity to close the bathroom door to do my business. So she did her business on the other side of the door.

Chaser was terrified of loud noises, other dogs, and all forms of public transportation, from buses to commuter trains. She was hand shy, shy around strangers – just plain shy.

Her expression was so darned pitiful. The Chicago police stopped me twice while we were walking, thinking she was stolen. She looked like a poster-pet for animal abuse.

Chaser liked my wife, Robin, fine. But she shadowed my every move. Today, as a dog behavior consultant, I'd suggest that Chaser was hyper-attached. When I moved somewhere she couldn't, everything inside of her came out, even when she was crated. No matter how often I took her out before I left the house, there was guaranteed to be a puddle and a pile when I returned home.

In desperation, whenever I left the house, Robin displayed an impostor kit to Chaser. She created a life-sized photo of me, draped an old T-shirt over it and played my voice on a tape recorder. Robin figured that if Chaser could see, smell, and hear me when I went out, she might be fooled.

She wasn't.

Two canine experts told me to give up on Chaser. I never considered that option.

You see, Chaser was a typical Brittany – so sweet. She would offer her heart on a silver plate to those she trusted if she could. It's a tough thing to articulate; feelings always are. I knew that Chaser unconditionally loved me, as so many dogs unconditionally love their owners. I knew her anxiety wasn't her fault. So I enrolled her in puppy obedience classes.

She was older than all the other dogs in class, but I thought puppy classes would be a great way for her to become more socialized in a non-threatening atmosphere, and boost her confidence.

We also spent months walking closer and closer to bus routes and trains, and meeting hundreds of strangers who presented Chaser with kibble I had stashed in my pockets. Finally, Chaser began her Pygmalion transformation into "My Fair Canine" when she earned her American Kennel Club Canine Good Citizen certificate.

A few days before being trapped inside the elevator, I was offered a position by Tribune Media Services to write a syndicated newspaper column. I had been writing about pets for years for the Chicago Tribune and various pet publications, but I was still dabbling at writing entertainment stories and general features.

Instinctively, I somehow knew that if I said, "Yes" to the opportunity, I would from then on out be cast as a pet writer and nothing else. I didn't know if I wanted to limit my career and myself. I thought it over. Sitting in the elevator … well, gave me time to think. And here's what I thought.

With all of her *issues*, Chaser was a wonderful dog. And if other people could benefit from this unadulterated joy, perhaps I should pass on to others what Chaser had given me. I never knew the human/animal bond could be quite like this. Intense but fun might be the best way to describe the relationship I had with Chaser.

Maybe things do happen for a reason.

I looked at my watch. It had been forty-five minutes since Blake first heard the elevator alarm. Lucy was curled up in my lap, and even Boots Montgomery had finally quieted down. I believe the other dogs picked up on Chaser's serenity.

Then it happened. Chaser, who was sitting only about six or seven inches away from me, got up and placed herself directly in my face. Our noses met. It was a moment that I'll never forget. It was the kind of moment that I always thought was reserved for Timmy and Lassie, or for some sort of pet psychic. At that moment I decided, yes, with absolute certainty, I should become a full-time pet writer.

Then, in a sort of restrained way, Chaser said, "Woof."

I can't claim to translate the woof, or that it meant that somehow Chaser approved of my decision. Then Chaser did what Chaser did best. She lay down and nodded off at my side.

Twenty minutes later, the elevator repair guy arrived to rescue us. His first question was, "What did you do all that time with three dogs?"

"We talked," I said.

Post Script: I did accept the newspaper position, and within weeks after that elevator experience, I wrote my first twice-weekly column. For all of these years, one of those two columns is a standard Q&A, with readers asking pet questions and me answering through some of the best experts in the country.

For twelve years, I hosted a radio show on WGN in Chicago. In 2009, I left that station and joined WLS.

For eight years, I've hosted two national radio shows. I've been a contributing editor at *USA Weekend* for several years and authored many pieces for pet magazines, for which I've written regular columns.

I've appeared on numerous national television shows, from *The Oprah Winfrey Show* to several programs on Animal Planet, to name a few.

I never dreamed of all this – becoming certified as a dog and cat behavior consultant, speaking around the world at veterinary and animal welfare conferences, and talking to the public and public officials on issues such as breed-specific bans. I'm honored to serve on several boards of directors, including American Humane, the Winn Feline Foundation, CATalyst Council, and Tree House Humane Society.

I've reached millions of pet owners, have impacted public policy, and I know my advice and counsel has saved lives. I wish I'd kept even a quarter of the emails telling me so. Those pets wouldn't have had help, at least from me, and I wouldn't have been given the greatest gift a person can receive – the chance to help others – if it wasn't for a Brittany named Chaser.

At the age of fourteen, Chaser was treated for mast cell cancer. She lived another year and a half, until the quality of her life faded. Of course, letting go is never easy. I know Chaser understood, or at least felt the love I had for her. What she sadly could never have understood was the impact she had on my life, and as a result, on so many other lives. All these awards I've received should rightfully have gone to her. Every day, I think about the lessons she taught me.

And every day, I miss her.

Steve Dale authors a twice weekly syndicated newspaper column (Tribune Media Services), and is host of two nationally syndicated shows (www.petwordradio.net), and Steve Dale's Pet World, heard on WLS in Chicago. He's also a contributing editor at *USA Weekend*. Steve's Web site is www.stevedalepetworld.com.

Chaser, "The Party Animal."

Image courtesy of Steve Dale.

My Dog: Speckles

Meeting Speckles

Speckles is a Brittany spaniel. I found him through a breeder who decided this was the last litter of puppies he would raise. He advertised the pups in a local newspaper.

My husband grew up in a family in which his father raised Brittany spaniels. "Some day," my husband once told me, "we will have a dog, and that dog will be a Brittany."

Several weeks before Christmas in 1995, I spotted the newspaper ad and responded to it. I wanted to surprise my husband with a Brittany for Christmas.

I traveled to the owner's house alone and looked at all the pudgy pups. Speckles struck my eye. He is orange and white and an attention grabber. He and one brother became my final selection. The breeder and I carried their wiggly bodies into the house, put them down, and watched them chew on an area rug. I sat on the floor and rubbed them as they raced by me.

Speckles had a narrow white line running up his forehead, forming a perfect heart shape on top of his head. His brother had a wide line running up his forehead and a dominantly white face. Speckles' prominent characteristic was his fear of being picked up. When his owner lifted him, he yelped until he was released. I found this peculiar, and I pitied the pup. I wanted him, but I would later let my husband make the final choice.

On our journey back to the breeder's home, I told my husband that I had a pup in mind. I would see if he felt the same way. We narrowed the choice to the same two pups and ended up with Speckles. He rode home on my husband's lap in the car. It was there, by observing the whining critter under the dome light of the car, that my husband decided to call him Speckles. Why? Because he has numerous orange speckles scattered on his nose and ankles.

A Crunchy Little Morsel

To Speckles, there is something fascinating about crumpled paper. This might stem from the playtime I spend with my cats when I wad up small pieces of paper and toss them across a tile floor for the cats to chase.

As for Speckles, he waits for me to throw a piece of paper into a wastebasket. Then he sneaks up to the basket, delicately takes the paper out, and tiptoes through the house away from me with the paper between his teeth.

Most often, I see or hear him doing this. He gets several feet away, and I will shout his name, or tell him, "You get back here!" Obstinate, he then takes off running and sits on the sofa with the wad of paper in his mouth, twisting his neck left and right as I try to remove the paper from his jaws.

When I don't hear him steal paper from wastebaskets, he proceeds to shred it up on the living room floor or sofa, waiting for my attention. Without my attention, he gets bored and leaves his mess for me to find later.

When he takes the cat's paper-wad toys, he quickly eats them so they can't play any longer.

His paper preference isn't limited to simple wads of typing paper. He will grab an old envelope, empty envelope box, or small magazine.

Still, I can't get him to carry in my newspaper. If he did, he would probably tear it to pieces.

Since he is such an avid paper thief, I have learned to crumple pieces of paper when he is several rooms away, so that he can't hear me do it. I tuck the paper wads deep into garbage cans and take out my trash often.

Despite the inconvenience of all this, I can't help but laugh when I see him saunter away with a wad of paper in his mouth. This normally klutzy pooch struts away with his head down. I can tell by the sound of his walk across wood floors that he has stolen paper and needs to be tackled.

Baxter Beagle

Over the course of Speckles' lifetime, he attracted a number of dog friends who would come to visit him outside of the fenced yard.

Speckles was so friendly; he was a magnet for every stray dog. Neighborhood dogs also seemed to pull their owners by the leash to my backyard so they could sniff noses with Speckles through the fence.

Every now and then someone with a dog buddy would move in next door to my house. A chain link fence divides my yard from that of my neighbor. Some of the dogs living next door would wiggle under the fence and come into my yard to play with Speckles. A few times Speckles squeezed himself under the fence and into their yard to run a lap or two before I spotted him.

One of the dogs I will always remember was Baxter Beagle. Baxter was a puppy when we first met him.

The little guy dug a shallow tunnel in one spot under the dividing fence and would shoot under it like an arrow when he wanted to visit with Speckles. Baxter could zip through it, but the tunnel was too small for Speckles to use and reciprocate the visits.

When I came home from work in the afternoons, Baxter saw my car drive along a side street, and he'd run across his backyard, dive into the tunnel and meet me at my garage side door when I came out. He was not only my neighbor's dog, but also apparently, mine.

I would open the backdoor to my house, let Speckles out to meet Baxter, and they would run and play outside for a bit. When Speckles was ready to come inside for his dinner, Baxter would sneak in behind him and run around inside my house.

One afternoon Baxter and Speckles ran laps around my sofa – making me laugh as I watched a white-tipped beagle tail circle the sofa, followed by a flash of an orange-colored Brittany. The whole time, they growled with delight.

Baxter used to play games with me, too. In typical beagle style, he would take things and hide them.

I would come home to find one or both of my gardening gloves missing. Baxter would visit my yard and enter my garage while I was away from home, steal my gloves and take them back home through the tunnel under the fence.

Time after time I'd find one of my gloves stuck on top of the chain link fence. My neighbor would find the gloves in his yard and place them on the fence top so I could retrieve them.

Then my gardening tools started to be raided. I came home at different times to find the spout on my plastic watering can chewed to pieces, the rubber handles on a pruning tool mangled and a ball of twine mutilated.

One day I laughed hysterically as Baxter took my hoe by the handle, dragged it across the backyard, and tried to pull it through the tunnel under the fence.

Speckles would watch these antics and pant with joy.

I had a small water garden in a wooden crate on my patio. Speckles would routinely drink out of it when he was warm. One day I walked by the water garden and Baxter was in the water – his floppy ears floating on the surface as he panted.

Speckles learned from Baxter and later decided to put his front legs and chest into the same watering hole to cool off.

Sometimes when he was inside my house, Baxter would take Speckles' stuffed toys and run to my back door. He took several toys outside and then home, under the fence. Speckles just allowed it to happen.

More than once I retrieved multiple stuffed animals that belonged to Speckles from Baxter's yard.

Bra Stealer

The one item of clothing that Speckles likes to hunt out of laundry baskets and clean stacks of laundry is my bras.

There is something about the motion they make when he swings them wildly by the straps that appeals to him. He hunts them out repeatedly. He also knows that by stealing them from me, I will come after him quickly to take them back.

His latest bra-stealing episode took place one evening while I was taking a shower. I heard a thumping sound in the living room, a bit of grunting and growling, and I knew he had taken something off-limits and was having fun shaking it to death.

I shouted his name from inside the shower, but he continued to thump around. When I was able to climb out of the shower, I peeked around the bathroom doorway into the living room and saw him, bra hanging out of his mouth, both cups meeting below his chin.

"What are you doing?" I shouted.

He kept on shaking and growling.

When I made it to the living room, he jumped onto the sofa and continued to hold the bra in his mouth, cups dangling. Torn between laughter and anger over my new bra being slobbered on and stretched out of shape, I reached out cautiously to remove it from his teeth.

He twisted his neck from side to side, up and down, and finally, released my bra.

He also enjoys snatching smaller items of clothing, such as socks, underpants, and washcloths.

I have thought of scolding him by putting a bra on him and making him appear in public that way, being ridiculed by neighbors and canine and feline friends. However, he would probably enjoy the attention.

So I continue to hide my bras inside other dirty clothes when I toss them down the laundry chute, and fold my clean bras right away when I finish cleaning a load of laundry.

Canine Turbo Chaser

I am slightly embarrassed to say that my dog likes cat toys, especially the circular turbo ball chasers that have a scratch pad in the center.

As a pup, Speckles was fascinated by the sound of the orange ball in our turbo chaser spinning round and round. He would slam his big paw down on the side of the ball, shooting it around, and then punch his nose down on the track after it.

He would try and try to bite the ball, attempting to take it out of the track. My husband and I would look at him and laugh, thinking this cat toy was the perfect pacifier that would give Speckles hours of fun.

Ironically, my cats seldom find that orange ball interesting and they rarely play with it. They mainly use the scratch pad.

This turbo chaser is now located in an office in my house. All of the cat toys are in this room, kept out of Speckles' normal play area because he'll take everything they have unless they're hidden.

While I was typing one afternoon, Speckles insisted on making that ball roar around the track until my head started to ache. To stop the madness, I plucked the ball from the track and rolled it through the house for him to play with. For several minutes he was in the living room with the ball, bouncing it off of wooden furniture and growling at it.

Then he ran back down the hall toward the office where I was working.

I figured he would shoot the ball around on the wooden floor while I was working, fueling my insanity again, but his following actions amazed me.

Speckles walked back to the turbo chaser, stood over it, dropped the ball onto it, then slammed his foot down on the ball, securing it back in the track.

He turned and glanced at me, then looked back at the ball and started shooting it around the track again. I was shocked and amazed at his intelligence. My cat, Desdemona, was sitting on a drawing table above him, staring intently at his actions.

At first I thought he wanted the ball out of the track. However, once I freed it for him, it wasn't as much fun. So he figured out how to put it back in the track.

I felt the need to commend his behavior by giving him a treat. Since that day, he hasn't touched the turbo chaser.

He has, however, stolen the cat's stuffed mice and furry balls and attempted to shred them, all this despite his collection of thirty-plus dog toys conveniently scattered about the house.

Cotton Fields

I noticed it one afternoon. Tufts of white, fluffy cotton started to appear across my lawn. Dead grass around those areas told the secret: these cotton tufts were leftovers from doggie poop. I paused to figure out what was causing Speckles to create this field of cotton.

Even though I do a ritualistic every-other-day pick up of the piles, some of them get beaten in by rain before I can catch them. Those leave the cotton behind. My husband then fillets it with blades of the lawn mower, spreading the field of cotton even further.

The source of Speckles' cotton diet was – I must use the past tense because the source has been disposed of – a quilt that lined his crate. This quilt, made in my childhood from scraps of my old clothes, became his possession after he soiled his wool and knitted blankies beyond repair. I won't get into the details of that ordeal.

That old quilt was just that – old. The more he slept on it, dug around in it, rubbed his nose in it as he buried bones and balls, the more it frayed and tore. Through the squares of fabric escaped quilt batting.

I can't figure out whether the smell of it, the taste of it, or the feel of it in his mouth made him want to continue chewing at it at night while we slept.

One afternoon I stuck my head into his crate, much to his dismay, and examined the quilt damage. I figured that I could continue to let him sleep on the quilt if I turned it over, exposing only the backside that wasn't fraying. He edged his way into the doorway along with me to watch me work. A few treats and a nylon bone were discovered underneath.

Days later the cotton field started sprouting again in my yard.

One morning I stood in the dew-covered grass waiting for Speckles to relieve himself. His squatting stance continued for quite some time and I noticed that tufts of cotton were causing constipation. I stood at a distance, squinting, trying to figure out if I needed to help him or if he could work it out himself. After several grunts, the cotton was free.

I immediately retired the quilt and chose alternate bedding.

I discussed his cotton-eating habits with a friend the other day. She told me that her golden Labrador leaves colorful piles around her yard quite often. One day he ate a plastic, disposable razor – all of it except for the blade. Chunks of plastic appeared across the lawn.

Speckles often eats things he isn't supposed to eat. He doesn't realize that I eventually find out what those things are. I find out either by evidence in the house or by evidence in the yard.

Drinker

My dog is a lush.

Yes. Speckles will drink anything from anywhere, anytime. A glass or can of liquid isn't safe in his presence.

A large ceramic tub with a water plant in it sits on my patio. Speckles can be heard sloshing his tongue in and out of the water periodically throughout the afternoon. I provide a bowl full of fresh water nearby, but he prefers the tub.

I think he likes this tub because it is about the same height as our toilet, which he dips his head into to get a drink.

One day I heard sloshing coming from the living room and I rushed to the scene. Speckles had his nose stuck into a drinking glass my husband left beside the sofa. It was half full of soda, but when I got there, the soda was nearly all consumed by Speckles.

My neighbor brought his golden retriever over to visit Speckles one afternoon. In the man's hand was a can of beer. I caught the man offering Speckles a lick, and of course, Speckles accepted.

Speckles has an unusual preference for iced tea. One evening after dinner, my husband left a glass full of tea sitting on the dining room table. Speckles put his front feet on the table and stretched his tongue out as far as he could, lapping tea out of the glass.

Every night after I have cereal for a snack, Speckles lies at my feet waiting for a *licky* of milk. When I am finished drinking all the milk from the bowl, he gets to remove the residue with his big, pink tongue.

Puddles, river water, dishwater from the kitchen sink, have all been on Speckles' beverage list over the past two years.

He especially enjoys a wading pool we found in an alley and patched for him so he could slosh around in it during hot summer days. Add a little ice to the pool water or his dog bowl, and Speckles is an especially happy boy. He sticks his nose under the water and hunts for ice cubes. Bubbles of air rise from his nose, intriguing him even more.

I must note one iced tea-drinking episode that sticks out in my mind. As a matter of fact, I never told my husband this. My husband left his glass of tea sitting on the dining room table one evening and I spotted Speckles helping himself to a drink. I didn't have time to pick up the glass, and my husband came back in and started drinking what was left. He was quenching his thirst so fast; I didn't have the heart to tell him what had happened.

Drool Toys

There's nothing like the slap of a dog-drool-soaked stuffed animal or sock against your face, bare leg or arm.

Speckles has favorite drool toys – a pudgy white duck named Duckie with an orange beak and feet, and various sockies. I have had an up-close and personal experience with each.

If I ignore Speckles, he will make me pay attention. Several times I have been eating dinner and the spongy duck ends up in my lap. If I take a nap on the sofa, a soggy size-ten cotton sock rubs against my cheek.

Dogs are peculiarly fascinated with absorbent toys and rubber balls. Take a look in any pet store and see what the popular toys are: rubber balls, squeaky toys and fleece or furry playthings.

It is evident that until the day a dog toy is made with a *dry weave* shield, soggy toys will continue to decorate my home, leaving wet marks on comforters and smudges on windows.

The tale of Speckles' duckie toy started at a garage sale. I spotted it in a bin, only fifty cents and thought of my pup. The stuffed animal looked sturdy: two securely attached eyes and no loose appendages. I took it home, washed it, tumble-dried it, and handed it to Speckles. He took an immediate liking to it, holding it by the neck, shaking it left and right, and tossing it in the air.

At night he leaves the duckie outside his crate door, just within his sight. Some mornings he takes it outside with him while he goes potty. A couple of times he's had an accident with it. One morning he dropped it in the grass and unintentionally peed on it.

Once again, Duckie went through the wash and dry cycles.

Another evening he played in the yard with Duckie while my husband and I finished some landscaping. Duckie's saliva bath became a magnet for dirt. Soon, he was soiled from beak to foot. Again, it went through the washing machine.

Speckles' soggy friend has been found in many places: between the sofa cushions, on the dining room table, on our bed, in the bathtub, buried in a box of old newspapers and stuffed on the bottom shelf of the refrigerator.

Several times Speckles broke his devotion to Duckie and hunted out my sentimental stuffed animals, such as Froggie and Bunnie. A small gathering of such polyester friends formed on the living room floor one evening. Speckles and I promptly had a talk.

All of his rubber and plastic balls he mangled into obscure forms.

A neighbor kid gave him a cartoonish-looking *squeezy ball*, as I call it, which he chews on until its insides are soaked in saliva. Then he brings the gift to me, squeezing it over my legs and arms until I have a shower.

Most of the time he drinks a full dish of water before bringing me his ball, thereby increasing the moisture flow.

Recently he discovered my cats' toys, including catnip mice. After he snatches them off the floor, I have to pry his jaws open to remove them. By that time, they are soaked beyond recognition. The cats, wise to his repulsive behavior, never touch the toys again.

Embarrassing Moments

I have this fear that Speckles will do something embarrassing in front of company. He's been known to pass gas silently, making everyone look at each other for an answer. But there are other habits he usually acts out when only my husband and I are home. I pray he will never do them when we have company.

If there is a dirty pair of underwear in the bottom of a clothesbasket, he will find it, bring it out, and play with it. Time and again I have found my husband's undies lying on the sofa, in the hall or on the kitchen floor.

The dog also has a fetish for nylon stockings. He sniffs them out of storage, carries them around, and pulls them through his teeth like bubble gum.

It would be grounds to end a house party if he ever pulled out a pair of underwear and started playing with it among visitors. I dreamed about this. Since then, I have made sure all forms of clothing are tucked into drawers and closets before company comes.

One of my ultimate nightmares took place recently while my in-laws were eating dinner at our house.

Just before they came, Speckles decided he'd play with his stuffed moose, which is nearly half his size. When he was younger, before he was neutcred, he thought this moose was a female dog and tried to mate with it. We took it away so he would stop. Since he is neutered now, I thought he would no longer wish to make love with the moose.

I was wrong.

While we were sitting at the table eating, Speckles was in the living room playing with his moose. My sister-in-law suddenly asked me, "Uh, is that normal?" and pointed at him. Children at the table swung around in their chairs to view him trying to mate with the moose under a floor lamp.

Immediately I ran across the room, snatched up the moose, threw it into a back room, and slammed the door.

Speckles enjoys pushing his limits with me. He knows this behavior gets my attention and I'll have to speak to him, even if it is a loud lecture.

I guess I shouldn't act as if he's a person or a family member and keep in mind that he *is* an animal. But I always feel that I have to justify his actions to everyone who questions them. When he hops like a cricket around people, I try to calm him and tell people, "He's just excited to see you." When he wanders around the dinner table while we are eating, I explain that he's only looking for a tidbit.

But how do you tactfully explain why your dog likes to play with dirty underwear, or why he drinks out of the toilet?

These are questions only dog owners seem to understand. Maybe there should be a support group for pet parents.

Everybody Needs Somebody, Sometime

Anyone who thinks or says that animals do not need humans for help is wrong. My dog recently proved this to me, in great detail.

I woke one morning to a strong smell – the smell left behind when one of my pets goes to the bathroom. I sat up in bed and saw both of my cats sleeping on either side of my legs, trapping me under heavy comforters. I lifted their tails carefully to see if they'd brought any little potty presents to bed with them. They looked at me with wide eyes.

I thought I heard Speckles whine from his crate a short time earlier. I fell back to sleep, and woke shortly before my alarm sounded to this suffocating smell.

With my eyes still foggy from sleep, I made my way to the living room where Speckles sleeps in his crate. He was leaning against his cage door, anxious to escape. I could see that his sheets were dirty and the odor was stronger than ever. He had pottied in his cage, and from the looks of it, vomited too.

My plan was to get him outside immediately, meaning that he would have to dash through the dining room and kitchen to get to the back door. He came out of the cage and wanted to put his feet up on me, a morning ritual, but instead I rushed him through the house. He shook from head to toe and flung waste on surrounding furniture, my bare feet, and my ankles. Finally, he exited the back door.

I knew he had to be bathed before I went to work, and so did his cage. The sheets needed to be disposed of, the furniture needed to be cleaned and finally, I had to find out if he was still sick.

A roll of paper towels, several garbage sacks, scented candles and bath towels later, the mess was gone. Speckles was lying calmly on the sofa, head flat against the cushions. He felt warmer than usual when I put my hand on his head. He looked at me, asking silently if I was leaving him for the day. I called my veterinarian and took him in for a checkup first thing. Speckles had a slight fever, and the diagnosis was gastrointestinal upset. He received a shot and medication for the night.

Since I had to work, I called my mom to come over and take Speckles outside later that day. She sat with him for nearly an hour, and he didn't potty or eat.

That evening, he still was lying motionless on the sofa. His stomach gurgled and churned with gas, so loudly that I could hear it a room away. He shifted from time to time, trying to relieve the pressure.

From the sound of his tummy, I didn't want to leave him in the crate all night for fear he would get sick again. So I slept on the sofa with him, wrapped up in a comforter. He lay beside me with his head on my chest and his nose tucked under my chin. He was warm, his nose was dry, and he desperately wanted to play. Once, he picked up a stuffed toy, brought it up on the sofa, and laid it beside me. He fell asleep once again.

Twice that night he woke and quickly ran to his crate. Most dogs, experts say, do not defecate or urinate in their crates, because their crate is their *home*. Speckles isn't like most dogs. He made a dash for the crate to vomit. The door was partly shut, and he banged his head on it trying to get inside. After the initial stun, he made his way inside, relieved himself, and then came back out to lie down.

After using another roll of paper towels that night and washing another load of laundry, Speckles went to the veterinarian again the next morning. This time, he stayed overnight for observation and intravenous fluids. I took his green *coo coo bird* squeaky toy with him so he felt at home. The thought of needles in his little spindly legs made me hug him tight before I left him. He sat on the cold, metal exam table, leaning against my chest. He looked up at me, tongue pulsating in and out of his mouth slowly. I kissed his forehead and surrendered him to the doctor.

Love and affection is the best treatment for any ill creature. With love, healing is quicker and the illness is easier for the patient to endure.

Before he left to stay overnight at the veterinary office, Speckles didn't leave my side. He knew I would hold him and make his pains go away. I relied on him through all the times he protected me from strangers and harmless squirrels passing through our yard, and now he relied on me.

Speckles came home from his overnight veterinary stay with no more fever and a hearty appetite. He rode home with his nose sticking out of my car window. When he entered the fenced-in yard, he ran several laps around it.

It felt good to have him home.

Friends Along the Fence

Speckles always had a personality that attracted children and adults to play with him. What struck me is how his spirited demeanor drew many four-legged creatures.

Any stray dog in the neighborhood seemed to end up at our house sniffing Speckles' nose through the chain link fence. They ran laps along the fence line with him chasing close behind.

I remember many canine visitors, including those living in the house next door, sharing a chain link fence, which divided our yards.

Baxter Beagle selectively zipped through a low spot under the fence and played with Speckles in our yard.

Leo, a golden chow chow, watched for me to come home from work every day and sat at the fence until I came to greet him. I lifted up the fence from the bottom, and let him into our yard to play with Speckles. When he was ready to go home, he'd stand at the fence. I'd lift the fence again to let him go back home.

A Yorkshire terrier named Buddy lived in that same home for a time. He also dashed under the fence to play with Speckles.

A few years later, a different family moved into that home. They had a boxer, a rat terrier, and a small mixed-breed. The small dogs slid under the fence to visit Speckles; however, they wouldn't stop there.

The dogs were so determined to run free that they eventually started digging along my fence line, escaping and running around the neighborhood. It was then that their owner anchored the fence down with a variety of metal and wood gadgets.

A male Lhasa Apso visited a family living in a home behind ours. Speckles stood silently at the fence, staring at this little dog. The dog barked incessantly at Speckles until his owners let him come to the fence so the two dogs could sniff noses.

Frequently in the mornings, I saw an older lady with a West Highland terrier walking away from my fence. Apparently, her dog stopped by to say "Hi" to Speckles.

A black Labrador named Maggie nearly pulled her master across my front yard so she could sniff Speckles through the fence. Speckles stood quietly, his stubby tail wiggling fast, until his lady friend came closer.

At first, when I discovered strange creatures visiting my backyard, I was startled. Then their visits became so common I accepted all of them as my furry nieces and nephews. Speckles watched the backyard from the windows. He let me know with whimpers and barks when someone was visiting. I let him out to play with them before they had to go home.

A few of the visitors wandered from neighboring homes when they slipped away from their owners. They hung around the exterior of the fenced yard until I brought them in for safety's sake.

A Rhodesian Ridgeback appeared one day and

stayed until his master drove by looking for him.

A pit bull-mix named Molly appeared more than once. After our first meeting, when I reunited her with her owners who lived a block away, I simply let Molly into the yard to play with Speckles while I called her parents.

Several dogs came and went quickly without me being able to identify their owners. Two husky-mixes chased Speckles along the fence one afternoon and dashed off.

A large male German shepherd appeared one evening, ran along the fence, and vanished.

Then there was Bosco, a beautiful, golden Labrador mix that visited a home across the street. She would dash across our front yard, make Speckles bark with excitement, and then come to the fence to kiss his nose before running back home

Of all these visitors, three strays stand out in my memory.

A mixed-breed shepherd ran loose for weeks in the town near my home. Animal control workers tried to catch him, to no avail. I saw this dog dashing around town from time to time. A fellow animal rescue volunteer told me the dog even jumped fences and got a female dog pregnant in her own yard.

One day I let Speckles out to play, returned to the door, and was shocked to see that shepherd-mix standing in my backyard. He jumped over my fence and into my yard just to fraternize with Speckles. I couldn't believe my eyes. When I walked out into the yard to talk to the dog, it ran, and leaped back over the fence in a flash. Speckles stood at the fence, amazed at the dog's agility.

Then there was a beautiful blue-and-white male pit

bull that visited one afternoon. Speckles played with the dog along the fence for a bit. I was able to reach over the fence and pet the muscular beast.

The pit bull showed up when I was cutting my lawn on a riding mower. Turning around, I saw Speckles and the pit bull playing in my yard.

I grew a bit concerned at the pit's desire to chase Speckles and nip at him. I wondered about the pit's history.

When I went to my backdoor to let Speckles into the house, the pit bull growled and cornered me. Thankfully, I had my cordless phone with me and squeezed into my garage with Speckles.

An animal rescue worker came to remove the pit bull and find its owner.

One of our favorite visitors was Logan, a white shepherd that weighed well over one hundred pounds. He was twice as tall as Speckles.

The first time he visited, he came into my backyard when I opened the gate. He loved Speckles, and they frolicked like brothers. His owner drove by in a van, looking for him, and thanked me for keeping him safe. Logan wandered to our home from about three blocks away.

That day, I wrote down the owner's name and phone number in case Logan appeared again.

Sure enough, Logan came back several more times over the years. He dug out of his yard or pushed a fence open to free himself. Each time, without fail, he came to our home to see Speckles.

More than once I packed Logan into my Ford Escort and drove him back home. He looked like a miniature horse sitting on my back seat and bracing his front feet between the front seats.

I always thanked Speckles for bringing these furry friends into our lives, if even for a few moments.

There is a biblical passage from Hebrews 13:2 that I think applies here – a passage that Speckles may have known in his heart:

"Do not forget to entertain strangers, for by so doing some people have entertained angels without knowing it."

Garbage Can Number 3

I remember coming home the first night Speckles decided to turn my kitchen into a ticker-tape parade route.

It was late, I was tired, and when I opened the backdoor, he greeted me calmly. After the greeting, he shot out of the backdoor and into the fenced-in yard. Strange, I thought ... he usually wants a little more lovin' before leaving me for a romp.

When I looked into the kitchen, I saw plastic bags, old melon rinds, cat litter, and other garbage on the floor. Rounding the corner into the kitchen, I saw the spill went on across the entire room. The garbage can lay on the floor on its side. In the living room was an old cat food can licked clean, and imprinted with several tooth marks.

It was too late to reprimand the dog. I cleaned up the mess, and then let him back inside the house.

As days went by, I devised a method – or so I thought – to avoid this happening again. I would empty a lidless garbage can as soon as it had anything in it that smelled good to Speckles. I started to go through garbage bags like water.

Still, he decided that papers smelled good, too. I found newspapers and paper towels scattered around the kitchen floor when I came home from work.

Next, I put the garbage can on a kitchen chair.

That, too, was a bad decision. Again, I found the can on the floor.

My next step was balancing the can on the back of the stove. This worked, but it became bothersome. Sometimes I even forget to place the can on the stove before I left home.

In desperation and sick of scrubbing my tile floor each evening, I went to a retail store and lined up one of each available rubber garbage can in the store aisle. I tested the lids, trying to think like a dog. I poked at the lids with my finger like a dog's nose would poke.

My choice was quick – a rubber can, the same height as my last one, but with a lid that flipped up by pressing down on a bar. He couldn't get his nose stuck in it, I thought. He couldn't press this bar and open it either, unless he was more intelligent than I thought.

So the battle continued. I set the can up and left it on the floor when I went to work. The first few times I came home, the can was scooted several inches from the original space. Then it happened again. I found the lid popped off. The spring mechanism lifting the lid by touch was broken.

This time the contents of the can contained shavings of candle wax that were now ground into my tile. I scrubbed the floor on hands–and-knees for half an hour.

The next day, I went to a retail store and lined up one of each garbage can on the floor, again. This time I found a taller can which featureed a half lid that rolled up by lifting a small lip. He couldn't possibly lift that lid without fingernails. And, the lid fit tightly, preventing the top from popping off easily.

When I came home with garbage can number

three, Speckles sniffed it inside and out. I lined it with a garbage bag and stationed it in the kitchen.

At first, I would come home and find it scooted several feet across the floor to the front of the sink or into the kitchen doorway. Still, the lid was intact and the roll-top was down.

Then it happened again. I was standing in the kitchen. I heard Speckles behind me bumping the rubber can. When I turned around, he had managed to lift the roll-top lid. He looked at me, and then ran into the living room.

I was stunned at his intelligence.

For a moment or two I stood and looked at the can. Then I closed the roll-top and pushed it with my finger, trying to figure out how a big pink nose could roll it up.

It didn't matter anymore, I told myself. I came home several nights later and the contents of garbage can number three were all over the kitchen. This can, too, gets positioned on the kitchen chair when I leave.

Hershey Bars

My dog likes to eat Hershey bars – not the sweet kind adorned with nuts or crunchies. *Hershey bars* is the code name my husband and I established for cat poop.

I don't understand why a pooch who gets his daily food requirements, countless bones as rewards, a weekly six-inch-long rawhide, and some table scraps needs to scavenge through scented cat litter to find these little dark treasures.

My husband and I figure they are rewards to him, like that delicious Hershey Bar we often crave in the afternoons. Thus, the code name *Hershey bars* evolved.

When I hear Speckles' toenails *tink-tink-tink* across the kitchen tile, I know he's on his way to a Hershey bar hunt.

My cat, Desdemona, seldom gets the pleasure of covering up her Hershey bars. I think Speckles can hear them drop in the plastic litter box, because he comes slinking into the kitchen.

I often wonder if he could hunt truffles or illegal drugs the way he hunts Hershey bars. He finds them in tall grass and piles of leaves when we walk together.

He hasn't figured out, yet, how I can tell he's been in the litter box searching for these delicacies. Sometimes I find litter residue lying in one area on the carpet, a sure sign he's been Hershey bar hunting.

Other times he comes walking up to me with litter clumped to the top of his nose. When I scold him, he doesn't understand why.

One afternoon I was standing outside our dining room window, and he looked at me through the glass. He disappeared, and then came back with scoopable cat litter clumped around the top of his wet, pink nose. He rubbed his snout around the windowpane, tongue dangling, and left a gray film gathered from litter. I shouted his name, and he ran from my sight.

One night I was in the kitchen and he stepped over to the litter box, looked at me, and then started to paw gently at the litter. I scolded him immediately.

Of course, he continues to test my patience. His paw prints can frequently be spotted in the litter.

My hope is that Speckles will grow out of this disgusting habit; but at the age of one, he shows no signs of stopping.

My husband suggested sprinkling the cat litter with ground pepper or hot sauce, but that will make my cats deposit their Hershey bars elsewhere.

The only positive side of all this is I seldom have to clean the litter box.

How Tall Am I?

I have learned Speckles is trying to show me that he is a member of the family by persistently reaching up to my height. Time and again, I find him standing on his back legs to see what I am doing at the kitchen and bathroom sink, washing machine, stove, windows, trunk of my car, and dining room table.

Plopping his big front paws on surfaces beside me is not a graceful act to watch, and probably wouldn't be accepted in most households. I restrict his foot-plopping habits, but he still sneaks up beside me to see what I am doing.

When I wash dishes, he pops up beside me with his feet on the counter. He watches the faucet run, often lapping at the soapy dishwater.

After feeding my cats, which eat on the kitchen sink, Speckles inspects the bowls by placing his paws on the counter. I usually hear his toenails clinking across the kitchen tile, and then suddenly stop. When he stops, I know he placed his feet on the sink and is looking around. When I call his name, a thudding sound follows (feet hitting the floor), and he slinks out of the kitchen.

Evidence that he inspected the cat food dishes is always clear. He reaches his tongue out as far as possible and licks at the food over the rim of the dishes. I find little bits of food flung against the wall, toaster, and counter top.

When I am cooking at the stove, he wants to see what I am doing. Placing his feet on the stove controls is a dangerous habit, so I quickly scold him verbally.

Speckles sometimes rises to my height and sniffs the toothpaste dispenser when I brush my teeth.

Standing at a window, I am accompanied by his short frame, extended several feet high as he stands on his hind legs.

Doing paperwork at the dining room table, his head and front feet often appear, so he can sniff my papers and scoot them off the table.

When I sit on the sofa, he joins me on the cushions.

After I throw away garbage, Speckles sticks his head inside the can to see what is inside.

Really, it isn't fair that he is short. He just wants to fit in with tall humans and not be stuck at knee height.

Sometimes I lie on the floor beside him and get a view from his perspective. It's chillier down there, and more intimidating to be surrounded by walls, bulky furniture, garbage cans, floor plants and appliances. I'd want a better view too.

Killer Urine

My front yard looks like a leopard's coat.

Since we have no trees or bushes, Speckles has to squat to relieve himself. Because he drinks so much water, lapping from the toilet and from the running bathtub faucet, these potty stops turn into torrential downpours on select areas of the lawn.

Before he was neutered, his urine didn't seem to bother anything green. But now that the *snip and clip*, as my husband calls it, has been performed, our dog has become a portable weed killer.

When we first moved into this house, our yard was full of weeds. My husband purchased a weed and feed mixture, applied it, and the lawn started to turn a fertile green. We filled in bare spots with seed patches, and the grass came back full and healthy.

Then along came Speckles. The first time he ever raised his leg to pee on a tree, I smiled from ear-to-ear with pride. My baby had finally reached manhood.

My uncle joked with us, saying that my husband should show Speckles how to pee on a tree. He claimed that our puppy didn't know how to be a *real dog* because he didn't have other dogs to show him this natural way of relieving himself.

My husband couldn't and wouldn't bring himself to wet on a tree just to teach the dog. He did, however, try to raise the dog's leg when he came to a tree. Speckles, fearing his leg was being twisted off, became alarmed and ran away.

After Speckles raised his leg the first time, he found joy in lifting his leg on everything vertical he passed. He didn't perfect his balance until months later, and I laughed every time he tried to raise his leg.

Two legs would go up, the front paw grasping the bottom of the tree, the back leg wrapping around the tree high above his back, and his chest leaning against the trunk. The stream would flow, his tongue would dangle, and his eyes sparkled with delight.

He used to pull me every time I took him out the front door, so he could christen one side of my neighbor's evergreen bush. As the lawn started to yellow, I noticed the bush starting to yellow, too.

I am intrigued by his intricate pattern of urination. He never pees in one spot twice. He ventures around, polka-dotting the yard with lakes, each lake killing the grass within twenty-four hours.

I was pulling weeds one afternoon and came across a plantain plant in the middle of a yellow patch. It, too, was dead, black and shriveled, and the root a mass of mush. I dug it up, and showed my husband.

He suggested we bottle the dog's urine and sell it as weed killer. I thought about training the dog to retain his urine and squirt each weed in an effort to save our lawn.

I asked my veterinarian, a pet store owner, and two lawn-care professionals if male dog urine should kill a lawn like Speckles' does. They said this was normal.

What could I do to stop it? Three out of four advised dousing each spot of urine with water when he was through.

My mother laughed at this advice, noting I would be in the front yard with a hose, or a jug of water, all day and night following my dog around.

I've tried to be this devoted, but I can't dilute every spot. When I see him urinating I stare at him with a jug or hose in my hand. His eyes question my stance.

Some may not see it, but when the grass is mowed and the spots are more evident, I think the dot-to-dot pattern Speckles draws resembles a tree.

I think he is trying to tell me something.

Learning To Be a Mother

The other day I grabbed a roll of paper towels and glass cleaner and decided to clean the dog nose prints off of my front door windows. It was obvious that even Speckles couldn't see out of the windows anymore because of the nose smears.

I sat on the floor inside, wiping the panes down and bopping Speckles with my free hand as he tried to eat the paper towel roll. When I was through, I went to the outside and sat on the porch to wipe the panes. He sat inside watching me.

When I squirted the window with cleaner, he jumped back. Then he started panting that *before the goofy mode* type of pant. I started wiping the window and felt a thump against the pane.

When I took the towel down I noticed him smearing his nose all over the inside of the window.

With each circular wipe I made, his nose went around and around. I could only see two flared nostrils and little front teeth. He pulled back. I put my towel up again, and he started rubbing his snout on the pane again.

I told him, "No," but it didn't do any good. He thought we were playing a game. I had to come back inside to clean the window again.

A lady I work with laughed at my learning experience. She told me I should have sought her advice before I started cleaning my windows with a puppy in the house. She learned how to clean windows from her child.

Being the mother of a toddler, she had a similar experience. After wiping the inside of one of her windows, she went to the outside to clean there, and found her daughter licking the inside of the window.

The moral of the story is: if you have a dog, wipe your windows from the outside and work your way inside.

I guess I could use some more of these parenting tips. My dog and cats act like children. It's fun and frustrating, learning their little games.

Speckles recently discovered the upright toothpaste dispenser on our bathroom sink. My husband had a habit of leaving the cap open after using it. The dog climbed up on the toilet seat with his front feet and licked the paste. This did wonders for his breath.

If we left the toilet seat up, he thought the toilet was a punch bowl, and sipped regularly as he walked by.

When I washed dishes, he put his front feet up on the sink and licked the soapsuds.

When I went to the basement to do laundry, a *thump-thump-thump* noise followed me. Speckles, afraid to come down the stairs since he fell through the open steps as a puppy, dropped his ball to me for attention. I tossed it back up to him, and he trickled it right back down.

When boredom would strike, he thumped around looking for something off-limits to grab, thereby, getting my attention. He didn't realize – or maybe he did and just defied me – that I have developed the ears of my mother, and can hear him getting into trouble before trouble happens.

There's the clicking of pens as one is plucked out of the pen holder by the phone; the crinkling of the garbage bag when he sticks his head into the can; and his toenails tinking on the kitchen tile before he puts his feet up on the sink.

One word, "Speckles!" rings out, and he comes strolling back in to see me.

I'll never forget the lesson he taught me about thawing meat.

One night I left a steak on the stove to thaw. I went to take a shower and told my husband to keep an eye on the dog.

When I opened the bathroom door after my shower, a hunk of empty aluminum foil was laying on the floor in the hallway. The dog was nearby licking his lips. The steak was gone.

Listening

Okay, I admit it. I have no control over my dog.

My husband gets mad at me when I don't speak to Speckles with force. Well, I am a small person. My voice doesn't get deep or sinister.

As a result, I am the one who gets scratched, walked on, jumped on, chewed on, and who receives any other signs of affection the dog desires to do to me. I say "No!" and he shakes his head, and then goes back to disobeying me.

The garbage can is his favorite temptation. Speckles always knows when I have my hands full of raw hamburger. Just when I get my hands full, he sticks his head in the garbage can and rummages around for loose cantaloupe rinds, empty cat food cans or dirty napkins.

I say, "No," stomp my foot on the floor, and walk toward him. He looks at me, steps aside, waits a minute, and then goes back to the garbage can.

I fear that his defiance will get him into serious trouble someday – like last night.

My husband was taking Speckles outside without a leash. Speckles stays in the yard if my husband shouts his name when he approaches the yard border.

Foolishly, I decided to take him out last night without his leash. I felt fairly confident that I could keep him in the yard. It worked a couple of times when I used treats as bait. But last night, Speckles wouldn't have cared if I swung a raw steak in front of him.

He knew my husband went across the street visiting my parents. He'd sat in front of the window, watched him walk over there, and he knew their front door was open, except for the storm door. He saw people walking around in the doorway.

The minute his potty time was over in the yard, Speckles took off running across the street to their house. When he arrived, he slammed himself into the storm door, rubbing his nose all over the glass, trying to get their attention.

My parents popped their heads up and my husband rushed to the door to find our furry son AWOL from our yard.

Consequently, Speckles had a sore rear end that night. My husband spanked him for being disobedient and led him home by the collar. He also put him in his crate for a short time.

My husband told me not to *coddle* him. But I can't stand to see any creature cowering or whimpering. Every time my husband scolds the dog, Speckles comes running to me – the pushover. I have found Speckles, more than once, curling up on my lap in defense.

Last night, Speckles was definitely scared of my husband's wrath. When he came out of his crate, he curled up on the sofa, head down, and eyes looking up. He wouldn't even respond to the word *treat*.

Later, I found my husband on his knees beside the sofa, kissing the dog on the nose, trying to get his son to understand. Still, Speckles was cautious of him.

With me, it's a different story. Speckles still sticks

his head in the garbage can, grabs my nylon stockings and runs with them, licks hand lotion from my arms and legs after I apply it and steals my shoes.

Today, he tried to grab the cat while I was holding her. I thought I'd use my husband's approach to discipline: grab him by the scruff of the neck, make him sit and tell him. "No!

The steps worked! But then Speckles looked back at me. His mouth was open, and he panted in my face with a happy little hound smile. I just laughed.

See, he doesn't listen to me.

Little Jokers

My pets have a knack for making me laugh. Every day, I can remember at least one act they have done that made me smile, laugh, or share with a friend. Speckles is the number one clown in the house.

I will never forget the day he became a vacuum cleaner when a box of puffed rice cereal fell off the kitchen counter, hit the edge of the garbage can, and spilled onto the floor. Speckles was nearby, waiting for his ritualistic *licky* of milk after I am finished eating my cereal.

A spring-like action sent him to the spill site, where he licked rapidly until every piece of rice was gone – almost all of it. Those only remaining pieces were stuck to the top of his warm, wet nose. He looked up at me for more, with his rice-coated snout, and I laughed to myself.

Speckles also has a knack for burying rawhide bones around the yard and in the house, then walking casually around the burial site, casting glances at me and back to the location until I question him about where the *bonies* are.

Recently, he circled a bushel basket full of begonia plants on my patio until I came closer to see why. I noticed that several begonias were missing and that the soil was thrown about. The top of his nose was black with dirt, and I knew what he had done. He watched me dig into the basket of begonias with my hands and unearth his bone. Then he took it and found another burial location.

In the house, he likes to stick these rawhides under clean laundry, dropping the bone in the center, and then lifting the clothes with his nose, up and over the bone. I find the bones later when I fold the laundry.

When I use the restroom, he barges his way into the room and jumps into the bathtub. Then, he stares at the waterspout until I turn the water on. He often prefers running water rather than water standing in a bowl.

I received a large tomato at work one day. I brought it home and placed it in the windowsill in my kitchen. While I was washing dishes one night, he stood beside me staring at the window. I asked him what was intriguing him and followed the tip of his nose to where it was pointing across the room. When I touched the tomato, he jumped with excitement. I know he loves vegetables, but he hadn't seen me put the tomato there. He must have spotted it across the room.

One afternoon I decided to make a grapevine wreath in my backyard. I cut long strands of wild grapevine hanging over my fence and Speckles stood by my side, watching. I tasted a grape hanging on the vine and offered one to Speckles. He took it willingly and started to beg for more.

When I twisted the vines on the ground, more grapes fell off and Speckles started sucking them up as they fell. Amazingly, he remembered where I picked the grapes and throughout the season, I found him along the fence, his head high in the vines rummaging for grapes.

I soon learned that grapes are unhealthy for dogs to eat, so I had to stop his grape-eating habit.

To my surprise, Speckles has now mastered the art of being a matador; however, his capture isn't a bull. It is a stuffed moose he has played with since he was a pup.

I heard a ripping noise one evening and looked into the living room. There, in the middle of an area rug was one of the moose's ears. It was a clean rip. No stuffing escaped. That ear sits on a table now. The moose's antlers were cropped off in a similar manner last year. Now, the moose has one ear, no bottom lip, remnants of yarn hair on the top of his head and a tail that hangs by several threads.

Little Things That He Does

I smile and laugh when I think of all the crazy antics Speckles has done over the last few months. I have recorded some of them to remember when he is older and less active.

First and foremost, I know he just does these things to get my attention. Every time he does them, he achieves this goal.

One evening I was cleaning my kitchen floor tile and moved most of the objects that were sitting on the floor out of the room. The garbage can was the last to go.

I heard a scuffing sound while I was in another room and came back to the kitchen to find him scooting the can around the kitchen with his nose. His head was bowed to the floor and his nose was at the bottom of the can, and he was pushing it in circles. When I asked him what he was doing, he stopped and looked at me like I should have known. Maybe he was trying to help me move the can out of the room?

In our new house, we have a laundry shute and several laundry baskets sitting under it in the basement to catch dirty clothes. Speckles learned this technique. He watches us drop clothes into the hole, then he runs to the basement and brings up a pair of underpants or a sock. He's selective in his choices of dirty clothing to play with. I just shake my head when I find a dirty sock lying under the dining room table or on the bedroom floor.

This past fall I was planting nearly fifty tulip and daffodil bulbs under a large pine tree in my backyard. Speckles was lying in the grass nearby, watching me digging dirt with my small shovel. After I dug several holes, he disappeared from view and I went about my business. When I heard a snort, I turned around quickly and found him digging out the bulbs I had just planted.

He froze when I told him, "Drop it", and he stiffened, begging me to chase him. A thick ring of mud was caked around his pink nose. When I stepped toward him, he ran across the yard and chewed up his catch. I lost five bulbs that day to his jaws.

For Christmas I created two trees made of large branches, wrapped tightly with white lights and red glass balls hanging from the branches with long strings of yarn.

When I didn't play with Speckles, he would walk across the room and bop the glass balls with his nose, making them swing wildly. He didn't settle with just one; he sent several swinging in motion before he ran off and I dove across the room to stop them.

Recently, he started picking up landscape lava rocks in our backyard and running with them in his mouth. When I try to get them away from him, he starts to chew on them, creating a grating sound like fingernails on a chalkboard. That sound sends my husband fleeing in the other direction.

Yesterday, Speckles came to me with something hidden in his large spaniel mouth. I could see it puffing out his cheeks.

When I heard him crunch it, I saw a piece of terra cotta fall to the ground, and I knew he had killed my angels. There were two small terra cotta angels I had perched on a milk crate the day before. In his mouth was an angel head. The bodies were missing.

I lured him to the back door with the word *treat*, then snatched the head from the yard where he dropped it. The back of its head was missing and I spotted the body across the yard. The second angel was lying near the milk crate, its head also broken off.

When my husband came home from work that night, he saw the angels on the dining room table where I left them. He didn't question what happened. He only said, "I see the dog got the angels."

Who else?

Moosel

When I was a freshman in college, my mom gave me a large stuffed moose for Christmas. The moose wore a scarf and stocking cap. That was 1988.

When I brought Speckles home in 1995, that stuffed moose was still in my life. Speckles found the moose and immediately grabbed it in his mouth. He was just three months old, and the moose was as big as he was.

That moose became his favorite toy. He slept with it, resting his head on it as a pillow. He took it into his crate to sleep beside it. He carried it in and out of the house. He shook it like a rag doll, rolled on it randomly, and, unfortunately, tried to mate with it.

The moose took many lashings from aggressive Speckles. I took the scarf and cap off of the toy so they would not get in the dog's way.

Speckles eventually tore pieces off of the moose. I would find an ear, antlers, bottom lip, tail, one eye and so forth.

Each time, I would mend the moose and dispose of the missing parts.

That moose got so dirty that I would have to wash it in the washing machine and then tumble it dry in the drier.

Speckles would actually stand beside the washing machine and watch me put moose into the machine. I had to explain to him that his toy had to take a bath.

He would then stand outside and sniff the air coming out of the dryer vent. I think he could smell Moose tumbling around.

If Speckles was sick and needed to stay at a veterinary office overnight, I always took his moose with him so he felt comfort.

Speckles grew to be sixty pounds in his prime. The moose was then a quarter of his size. The poor toy was permanently soiled; it had missing parts and large stitches where I had repaired it with strong upholstery thread.

My mom told me a couple of times, "I think it's time to get rid of Moose."

But I promptly replied, "I can't. It's his favorite toy. He loves Moosel."

He had his moose all of his life, and I still have Moose today, over twenty years later. It reminds me of Speckles, and my cats still like to curl up beside it from time to time.

Moose will surely bring comfort to the next dog that enters my life.

My Spot

One afternoon I sat down on my living room floor, in front of my television, to eat lunch.

Slowly I felt the presence of a large form beside me, hovering over my right shoulder. When I looked up, Speckles was sitting on my cedar chest, peering over my right arm and down onto my plate. His pink lips were flopping in and out from his gums with every breath, the tip of his pink tongue pulsating slowly through his parted lips and his ears had fallen forward, up and over his eyes.

He was staring at my sandwich so intensely that I was able to wiggle my finger across the tip of his tongue and he didn't move.

The top of the cedar chest became his favorite sitting station. When I sat on the floor and watched television, he sat on the cedar chest beside me, pawing at my shoulder for a scratch on the chin or chest.

When I sat on the end of the cedar chest to watch television, he sat on the opposite end, then snuggled up close to me and placed his paw on my shoulder.

At night, we sat on the cedar chest together in darkness. He watched out a large picture window in front of the cedar chest and I rubbed his chest. Sometimes I combed his long ear hair. When he looked to the left, I looked with him; when he looked to the right, I looked the same way. He felt satisfied when I was through, leaping to his feet and running to his crate to sleep.

The cedar chest was also his lookout station, both when I am home and when I am gone. He stands in the center of the cedar chest, placing his feet on the windowsill and watching me leave for work. When I come home, he is standing there watching my car pull into the driveway. Sometimes, when I enter the driveway I see just the top of his head because he is sleeping at his post.

I keep a small blanket on the top of the cedar chest for him to sit on. When I come home after work, that blanket is rumpled into a ball, a sign that he has jumped on and off of his seat all day long.

I think that every pet has its favorite sitting station, and they will defend it. My mom's dog, Sugar, likes to stand in the seat of a living room chair with her feet on the arm, looking out a window.

My cat, Desdemona, likes to lie on the top of her scratching post in front of the living room window.

Occasionally, Desdemona will lie on the cedar chest to take a sunbath. In defense of the cedar chest post, Speckles will bounce around the chest until Desdemona moves.

Then again, sometimes Speckles will share his post on the cedar chest, sitting beside Desdemona while they both watch passersby out the window.

Mysterious Happenings

My friend, Jo, told a story once about her cats. She came home from eating dinner at a restaurant with her husband. She had brought home a good-sized piece of leftover steak. She put it on the kitchen sink for a just a few moments. When she returned, it was gone.

No traces of that steak were found. Not one cat was licking its face. Not a whisker on any of her cats was dirty.

She never found the steak.

We joke that it was dragged under a piece of furniture somewhere, and like a pack of hyenas, her cats devoured it.

When you own pets, these mysterious things often happen.

I tried to put on one of my tennis shoes one day and I felt resistance at the toe of the shoe. I had worn the shoes within the past twenty-four hours, so I couldn't figure out what was wrong.

When I tipped the shoe upside down, out rolled a very small pencil. I stood there laughing, wondering which one of the cats decided to place this gift in my shoe and push it way up into the toe so I could not see it. I also wondered where they found that pencil.

My mom and dad learned quickly that if they brought home a soft drink or a milk shake from a fast-food restaurant, and put that cup on a table or the kitchen sink, it would be stripped of its straw within minutes.

Their cat, Pooper, has a fixation for straws. He can delicately take one out of a drink container, not making a sound. He does this trick so carefully that he never knocks over a cup in the process. That is an amazing fete for a cat that weighs nearly twenty pounds.

One time I was visiting a friend and looked at a basket of fruit on his sink. I laughed, making him wonder what was wrong.

In the basket was a blue rubber ball that belonged to his Dalmatian. The ball had been carefully placed between apples and oranges. I asked my friend if he put it there.

He had not. His dog apparently plopped his feet up on the sink top at some point and positioned the ball in the fruit basket.

Which leads me to a story about an odd occurrence at my house with my dog.

One evening I came home after dark, and Speckles did not meet me at the backdoor. Instead, I heard voices from my living room.

Initially I was scared a bit since I live alone. I called for Speckles immediately, and he trotted to the backdoor nonchalantly.

I think I picked up something heavy with which to hit a possible intruder, but realized that if someone had broken into my house, Speckles would not have been so calm.

When I walked into the living room, the television was on. I didn't leave it on when I left home.

I looked around the room and noticed a blanket I

had covered the sofa with was rumpled up. In the middle of it was the television remote control.

I then laughed at Speckles, who apparently made himself a comfy bed on the sofa, rolled on the remote control and turned the television on.

What was he watching? Of all things – Animal Planet.

He could have done this by accident, but I think, knowing Speckles, I should just accept the extraordinary incident as one of his many secret talents.

Passing Of The Air

Pet owners have all experienced it: pets passing gas.

The silent ones are the killers. Usually this happens when a group of your family members or close friends is sitting around watching television. The odor wafts among you and each of you looks at the other questioningly.

Speckles' latest passing of the air was when my mother-in-law and nieces were visiting. A box fan and an extra open window were required to diffuse the situation.

I have learned that my dog's nose is the monitor to when these little air passings have been made. Usually, he becomes alarmed and sniffs the air himself.

Now, unfortunately, we can hear the odor coming. My husband didn't believe me until the other night.

It never fails that when Speckles stands with his feet on the dining room windowsill, he will let out little poutzes (as my grandmother always called them). Alarmed at the noise behind him, he shifts around, moving in circles, sniffing the air.

Embarrassing moments abound when he stands beside us at the dinner table and lets out a rash of little *duck calls*"

I had heard of other people's dogs passing gas, but I never experienced it until I had a medium-sized dog.

Dogs, however, shouldn't get all the blame for

flatulence.

Cats are culprits too. I had never heard them pass gas until my mom's cat, Pepper, stood on the kitchen sink behind me. I was digging ice cubes out of the freezer at the time and heard him toot. When I turned around, he stared at me, and then ran through the kitchen, leaving me with the aftermath.

Speckles doesn't stop with passing gas; he is also an expert at belching.

Often he does it in my face after jumping into my lap. Other times he will sit calmly nearby and let out a beer-guzzling-aftermath type of belch.

I still turn red when company visits and odors suddenly fill a room. I say it was the dog, but I wonder how many people honestly believe me.

Pumpkin Eater

Speckles has always loved fruit and vegetables. It could be because he watches me eat fruit and veggies and believes that anything I eat tastes good. I share them with him and he accepts with excitement.

Then again, I have found him willingly sneaking grapes off of a vine along my fence and picking tomatoes off plants on my patio.

One October I brought home two big pumpkins and placed them on the kitchen floor to carve.

Speckles circled around them, sniffing the fruit and watching intently.

He picked a spot in the kitchen doorway and lay down to watch me. His head tilted left, then right with question, and his tongue dangled gently from his mouth.

I started carving and placing pumpkin rind and guts on a newspaper beside the first pumpkin. The smell of the fruit filled the kitchen.

Speckles rose and began circling the pumpkins and me, watching and sniffing the air.

Out of curiosity, I let him smell the pumpkin I was carving. Speckles proceeded to lick it. By now I had removed the top cap and hollowed out the center.

Speckles continued to lick the outside of the pumpkin and before I knew it, he stuck his entire head and part of his neck into the hollowed-out shell.

I sat there watching him and laughed – my orange-and-white Brittany sticking his head in an orange pumpkin. He pulled his head out with pumpkin goop stuck to his furry ears. Then he plunged his head in again.

By now I was fighting to keep his head out of the pumpkin while I was carving the eyes and mouth.

When the first eye popped out of the hole, it bounced across the floor. Speckles saw it, grabbed it in his teeth, and ran out of the kitchen.

I continued to laugh as he came back into the kitchen, lay down beside me, and waited for the next eye to pop out of the pumpkin. When it did, he stole it and ran out of the kitchen.

When I was finished carving the pumpkins, I went into the living room to see if he had eaten the pieces he stole. He chewed them and left them all over the carpet. I laughed at him while picking up his mess.

The following years he enjoyed our pumpkin-carving adventures just the same.

I also learned that he enjoys pumpkin pie. I always save him a bite-sized piece and let him lick the residue from my pie plate.

Scrubber Destruction

My mesh bath scrubber is deformed, thanks to Speckles.

It all happened because he is jealous of my cat, C.D.

The scrubber destruction took place one afternoon when I was home on my lunch break. A quick pit stop in the restroom before returning to work encouraged C.D. and Speckles to join me. When this happens, they both jockey for position in the room.

Speckles is afraid that C.D. will hit him, and C.D. is afraid that Speckles will step on her.

C.D. walks up to my legs, rubs on them, and then jumps onto the edge of the bathtub so she is the same height as the dog's head. All the while, I, of course, am sitting on the toilet trying to avoid any fights that might sandwich me up against the wall.

If I pet them both, one with each hand, then Speckles sits down beside my left leg and C.D. sniffs Speckles' head while sitting on the tub ledge. Sometimes she will reach out her paw and touch him lightly on his back.

On this day, C.D. wanted to sit on the floor beside my left leg and Speckles couldn't reach his usual sitting station.

While I was petting C.D. and not acknowledging the dog, Speckles stuck his head over the bathtub ledge and grabbed my bath scrubber with his front teeth.

I didn't realize what was happening until I looked up and saw Speckles walking backwards out of the bathroom door with my mesh scrubber stretching out from a bathtub faucet handle to his mouth in the hallway.

Caught between laughter and frustration, I had to leap up and grab my scrubber before it was completely ripped apart. This, of course, helped him complete his goal – getting C.D. out of the bathroom so he could be close to me.

For a short time after that, I still used that mesh scrubber even though it looked like an unruly ball of yarn. And Speckles, with his incredible memory, still sticks his head over the bathtub ledge to grab that scrubber for attention.

That'll Teach Ya!

My husband doubted my dog's intelligence.

I observe Speckles more closely than he and learn more about his I.Q. every day.

Take, for example, Speckles' ability to sneak items away from me without warning. I call it the *bait and switch*.

I first noticed this act when I opened the refrigerator door one day. Usually he walks up to the shelves and sniffs around while I grab what I need. If his snout gets too close to something, we have a discussion.

One day he came into the kitchen with a squeaky toy and was roughing it up on the floor beside me. When I opened the refrigerator door, he walked up to the shelves with the toy in his mouth, still squeaking it, laid it on the shelf and walked away with a package of hotdogs in his mouth.

My eyes were on the squeaky toy, not the wieners. I did a double take before I realized what he had done. I rescued the wieners.

Several days later, he conducted similar acts with his stuffed ducky toy over a basket of clean laundry. I was folding clothes and he was shaking his ducky nearby. He circled the basket, placed the ducky inside, and walked away with two socks and the ducky.

Amazing.

When I sit at the dinner table, he usually sits beside me and rests his chin on my knee, looking at me with sad eyes. He has learned that if I ignore him, he can put his toys on my lap until I get so frustrated I have to throw one across the room.

He also enjoys rutting in bed covers and blankets. While he is rolling around and I am showering him with tons of baby talk, he pokes his nose deeper to find a shirt or sock and then runs through the house with it in his mouth.

My husband didn't believe me when I told him that Speckles does these things. Last night, I proved him wrong.

We were folding laundry and took a short break. Speckles circled around with his ducky in his mouth. Closer to the basket he came, and I whispered to my husband to watch him. Speckles put his ducky in the basket and took off running across the room with both the ducky and a shirt in his mouth.

My husband laughed and shook his head. I reconfirmed that my husband was the one who chose this gifted canine, a claim he quickly, and jokingly, disputed.

The Bruising Habit

My dog has a bruising habit.

Speckles grabs one of my husband's sneakers by the tips of the laces and swings it from left to right, like an elephant swinging a trunk. The longer the laces, the greater his fascination with this game.

The shoe flips over his head one way, then back over the other way. Each time it pelts him in the opposite side of the face. But that doesn't bother him. The simplicity of this game makes him more interested. He grunts and groans with delight.

When company comes over, he decides to swing this sneaker as he runs through each room in the house. We all have bruised knees to prove it.

Now, whenever we see him coming with that swinging sneaker, we move arms and legs aside.

One morning he decided to grab a wet, grass-covered sneaker out of a shoe rack, swing it through the living room like a crashing plane and bang it on an uphill swing into my cereal bowl.

After my milk bath, I changed my clothes before work. Then I decided to take the leather and lace ammunition away from him.

His sad eyes and sagging wet tongue broke my heart. That's the sweet curse of pets. They can eat a steak off of a table, dig a hole in a flowerbed or pee on a Persian rug, and we continue to smile. Later that day they'll lean against your ankle and you'll love them again.

Speckles searched for another shoe and came up with a leather one. Since he had de-insoled many of my husband's dress shoes already, I tackled him, took the shoe away, and pacified him with the sneaker once more.

I'm sure we all have pets with these weird habits.

Speckles, I'm embarrassed but proud to say, can de-insole a shoe in a split second. All of our shoes left on the floor or within nose distance on a dresser top, have had their insoles removed. My husband and I sat and watched Speckles' de-insoling process one evening just for fun.

In goes his snout up to his eyes, and out comes the foam. Once the insole is on the floor, he moves on to find another shoe.

I have also laughed over the positions he finds to lay and sit in while operating on these shoes. One day he was lying with his hindquarters up to his belly on the sofa, and his chest to his nose sagging down to the floor. Of course, his nose was in a shoe.

Of all the dog toys we buy him, a shoe satisfies him the most, followed by a plastic ball the neighbor kids threw to him and he wouldn't surrender, old socks, a nylon bone, a softball and a baseball we found in a street, an occasional pair of underwear and catnip toys he steals when the cats aren't looking.

You can never predict what a pet will take a liking to. Once they decide on an object, find a safe version of it that you can sacrifice or buy them a cheaper version. Then let them have-at-it. Their happiness brings us happiness.

The Great Bone Mine

Speckles loves rawhide bones. The ones with the knobs on the ends take longer to devour, so he prefers the long, circular ones that are easy to gnaw, like a Popsicle, right down to his paws.

He also protects them diligently.

I never give him one when he is outside. He won't bury it or lay it down when he's through chewing on it. He demands to take it back into the house and put it away – away in places where only *he* knows they are stored. He'll whine and grunt until we grant him his wish to go inside. Then we must leave him alone until his storage site is found.

When he was younger, Speckles hid biscuits this way. I would give him one. Later, I'd find out that my husband had already given him one. This went on for several days. We thought that he was eating the biscuits until I started finding them around the house. They were under beds, as far under as his hind-end could fit. They were in cardboard storage boxes. They were in closets that once were open and eventually shut before the biscuit was removed.

I often wondered if he could remember where he put these treasures, since I found them more often than he did. Then one day he proved me wrong.

I was folding clothes in our spare bedroom when his nose started to twitch and he began to snort. He ran straight for a bottom dresser drawer, and he began sniffing the whole perimeter.

Thinking that a mouse had worked its way into the dresser from behind, I was leery about yanking the drawer open. By now, Speckles was bouncing around, sticking his nose through the drawer crack, and pulling it open further.

"What's in there?" I asked him, yanking the drawer open half way.

He managed to work his way to the bottom of the drawer with his nose, digging with his front paws, tossing jeans and shirts in the air. I stood back, observing.

Up came his head with a large biscuit in his mouth.

My husband must have left the drawer open one day and Speckles tucked the bone into this inconspicuous place.

Today, Speckles' bone-hiding techniques are nearly perfected. Sometimes we find him burrowing in a wooden box of old newspapers, placing the bone or biscuit underneath. Other times he'll wander away from us with a bone in his mouth, take it to the sofa, and nuzzle between the cushions to leave his treasure.

Never will he bury a bone in his crate. The crate he has turned into a toy box for three tennis balls, a softball, a baseball, a nylon bone and several socks. If you enter his crate domain, he'll become hysterical. He'll push his way under your arms and get into the crate before you do.

Our late night entertainment comes when we tell him, "Get your bony!" He sniffs the whole house, bringing us bones, trying to figure out which one we are referring to.

The Toy Drop

Most of us lead busy lives these days and find it hard to give everyone close to us, including our pets, the attention they need and deserve.

Take my dog, for example. Speckles always finds a way to get my attention, no matter how busy I am.

His most successful tactic is climbing onto my bed and dropping stuffed toys onto the floor around my feet. Usually he does this in the mornings while I am ironing my clothes and trying to get ready for work. He hops around on the bed with a toy in his mouth, growling with delight and rumpling up my bed covers. Then he flips the toy onto the floor and lays his head flat on the bed, staring at the toy on the floor.

Sad eyes look up at me, then back to the floor, begging me to pick up the toy and toss it to him on the bed.

When he first did this, I felt sorry for him for dropping the toy while he was up so high on the bed. So I made his life easier by tossing the toy back up to him. Thus, I taught him I was a sucker every time he did it.

One time I didn't pick up the toy, so he went to his toy box and brought another stuffed critter to the bed and dropped it at my feet. This process continued until four stuffed toys rested around my feet.

My husband witnessed this toy-dropping game

once and didn't respond to Speckles' behavior. I had to explain to him that this was a game, and that the human must pick up the toy and toss it back to the dog on the bed.

Speckles' other favorite toy-dropping routine comes when I am doing laundry in my basement. He stands at the top of the stairs and drops a ball down the steps. If I don't pick it up for him, he charges across the concrete basement floor and finds the ball, scoots it all over, eventually loses it under something, whines persistently and I have to pull it out.

He expects me to toss that ball back up the stairs, where he immediately drops it back down again.

The Worm Eater

One day I was working in the front yard and Speckles was frolicking in the grass beside me. I noticed a night crawler wiggling around on the sidewalk.

From across the yard the dog hopped, pointed at the worm with his nose, and before I could move to stop him, he sucked it off of the sidewalk.

Now I could have stuck my fingers down his throat to dig the worm out, as I do to retrieve wads of paper, pen caps and various trinkets he steals, but the thought of grabbing that slimy worm made me hesitate that day.

The dog smacked his lips, licked his nose and the worm was gone. It must have tasted good, because similar events followed.

Several days later, Speckles was in the front yard with me. It had rained the day before and worms were surfacing. Speckles, being a hunter by nature, was nosing his way across the lawn, snorting every so often, trying to suck a worm out of the ground.

I yelled his name, he shot me a quick look with his nose covered in mud, and he went back to foraging.

Just when I thought he would outgrow this nasty habit, it got worse. The other day he stood on the sidewalk, nose pointed to the ground, head twitching to-and-fro and zapping out his tongue to pick up ants – big ants.

One night I went to take a shower and found a centipede in the tub. Speckles spotted it, hopped in, and sucked it off the tub floor.

Stray flies have buzzed our heads while we're eating dinner. Speckles chomps them right out of the air.

Last night a moth flew through an open kitchen window and into my face. My cat, Desdemona, spotted it and started dancing around the kitchen. Stove burner covers went flying through the air, and her tail brushed through hot, scented wax. The dog started to mambo with her, flipping his water dish over and biting at the air.

Eventually, while I was holding the cat under one arm and several breakables under the other, Speckles cornered the moth with his nose up against the wall. Fortunately, I was able to prevent him from eating this insect.

I wonder ... is it boredom that makes Speckles want to eat bugs and worms? Or is he just playing with them like he does with the cat, not realizing how big his mouth is?

With the cat, he often puts his mouth around her neck or bites her ears.

Of course, this is a dog that eats peas, peaches (an entire one once – pit and all), salsa, litter box waste and foam rubber, among other delicacies.

One thing I know for sure is that anyone who receives a kiss from Speckles is in for a big surprise. Few people know what has been in his mouth.

Their Bond

My ex-husband, Brad, didn't see Speckles very much when we were still married. He worked in a different state and came home on weekends to spend time with us. Spending time to bond with me was just as important to Brad as bonding with Speckles.

Brad and Speckles took car rides into town and drove by my parents' house, or they would go to the gas station to get something to drink and Speckles bounced around in the backseat waiting for Brad to return. They also drove to a nearby forest preserve and went for walks together.

In the summer, they walked across the street from our home to a river where Speckles ran along the riverbank picking up sticks, peeing on every tree and running top-speed through a park area. It is a private park, so Brad let Speckles off of his leash and the furry child stayed close to his master.

When they took these little trips together, I missed them both. Speckles knew me better than his *daddy* because I cared for him every day since we first got him when he was three months old. I fed him. I gave him fresh water. I washed him. I gave him medication and trimmed his nails.

When Speckles came back home, he would always run full speed through the house to find me. He wiggled with excitement, trying to tell me the fun he had just had with daddy.

Brad and I both shared a ritual with Speckles. This ritual was the *licky* of an empty cereal bowl. We would leave a few drops of milk in a bowl for Speckles. He expected his treat every morning and sometimes at night. Speckles learned to lie on the floor within arm's reach and wait until he was told okay or licky. Sometimes my husband would forget that Speckles was behind him waiting to have his treat, and I would have to remind him of the ritual.

Near the end of our marriage, Brad and Speckles created a new ritualistic time to share together.

It was a cold night, just before winter snow fell, and the ground was crisp with frost. Brad went outside and Speckles followed. Nearly one hour later, they hadn't come back inside. I thought they took a ride to town, but when I looked out a window into the backyard, I saw flames coming from a fire pit there.

Bending down beside the fire was Brad. I could see the shadow of his form against the flash of the flames. Next to him was Speckles, sitting and resting against Brad's leg. Brad was patting him on the back. They both were warm and the night was quiet with stars and the moon shining above.

Several weekends during the winter I found them sitting together near the fire. I knew not to disturb their time together, though they looked so peaceful that I thought about joining them.

The bond between them grew, and I haven't tried to take Brad's place beside the fire pit with Speckles. Sometimes Speckles walks around the fire pit during the day, sniffing the area where they sat.

Things He's Eaten

One Friday I treated myself to a box of soft-baked blueberry snack bars from a local store. I brought them home along with many other groceries, opened one bar (each was wrapped in a foil-type paper), and ate it in front of Speckles. I even shared a bite with him, since he loves fruit.

He watched me place the box of bars in a dish drainer basket on the sink – way at the back, out of paw and nose reach. He watched me eat two more bars over the next day and each time put the box back in the drainer basket.

One day I took a bar out of the box and did not share it with him. Instead, I packed the bar up with other items I needed to take with me in my car that afternoon.

When I returned home, the scene I found was impressive – so impressive that I stood for several minutes examining the evidence.

I knew a mess waited for me when Speckles met me at the back door as I arrived. He usually makes his getaway quick when he's torn something up, eaten something or pottied on the kitchen floor. That day, he nearly knocked me down trying to get out the door.

The remaining blueberry bars had all been removed from the box and carefully pulled from each individual foil pouch. Somehow, with his large paws and teeth he pulled the seam on each packet along the entire length until the bars were exposed. I didn't find one piece of paper or foil. Just perfectly torn pouches.

Speckles had consumed nearly every crumb of the blueberry bars, except a few pieces that blended in with the dark tile on my kitchen floor. Those bits of evidence he stepped on and squished into the floor.

At that point in Speckles' life, I had been writing down all the things he had strategically "gotten into" on the sink over the years and eaten. That list, below excludes the many times he was able to hop up and down like a child while placing his front paws and legs on the sink surface and reaching the cat's dry food bowl. With enough hopping and grunting he was able to tip the bowl, distribute all the crunchies on the floor, and lick them up.

Here's the partial list:

1 raw steak left in aluminum foil on the stove, in preparation for cooking,
12 marshmallow Peeps in the shape of bunnies, followed that same year by
6 marshmallow Peeps in the shape of gingerbread men,
20 small peat pots I planned to plant seeds in,
1 box of instant potatoes,
1 loaf of bread, followed by half of a loaf at a later date,
4 English muffins,
5 blueberry bagels,
1 packet of flavored instant rice mix,
1 packet of flavored fettuccine Alfredo noodle mix,

1 small packet of Gummi Bears,
1 package of Chips Ahoy (extra chocolate chunk) cookies.

Speckles' taste for fruit and vegetables has pretty much prohibited me from planting vegetables in the backyard.

I often find him sticking his nose into grapevines along the fence and pulling ripe grapes from the vines. He also watches me pick red raspberries and licks his lips, waiting to sample one.

This year I grew one tomato plant in a pot on my patio. I staked the plant up straight and watched it flourish, producing little green tomatoes. The first one turned ripe late in the season and I picked it – a perfectly round tomato the size of a baseball. I placed it on a lawn chair by my back door and went back to the yard to do some other gardening.

Something made me look up from my chores. I saw Speckles standing across the yard with something red sticking out of his mouth. He saw me look at him and he froze, the kind of reaction he has when he wants to tease me and run away.

"What do you have in your mouth?" I asked him.

When I started walking towards him, Speckles jumped and quickly consumed my tomato, stem, and all.

I watched two other green baby tomatoes on the plant and hoped they would mature. One day Speckles was nosing around the plant, sniffing the stem, and ripening fruit. I scolded him and he ran.

The next day, my two green tomatoes were gone, picked perfectly clean from their stem.

I know who was to blame.

Tiny Bubbles

When I was younger, I had a Labrador-mix dog that was possibly the most hyper canine ever created. We called him Wiggles. I'll never forget the holes he dug all over our back yard and the way he bit at our toes when we were barefoot.

One thing we always did for him in the summer was put ice cubes in his water bowl while he was outside in the hot weather. Wiggles enjoyed lapping the water and chewing the cubes.

Recently I decided to give Speckles some ice cubes in his water bowl. That afternoon, his tongue was hanging low and his sides were heaving as he tried to survive the one-hundred-degree weather.

He watched me open the freezer door, twist a tray of cubes, and drop a couple of cubes into this dish. He rushed over to watch them float, and while his attention was diverted, I walked to the sink to fix a bite to eat.

From across the room I heard the sound of water bubbling. When I turned around, Speckles was staring at the water dish. Thinking that I was just hearing things, I went back to my task. Again, I heard bubbles. When I cast another look his way, he had his nose under the water, exhaling.

He'd plunge his nose into the cool water, swish it

around bobbing for cubes, and breathe out several seconds while under water. I had to share this moment.

While laughing hysterically, I walked into the next room to get my husband, who was also looking around trying to figure out where the bubbling sound was coming from. We walked back to the kitchen to watch our little scuba diver.

Since the day we introduced Speckles to water and cubes, he runs to the kitchen every time he hears an ice cube tray being twisted. If a stray cube hits the floor, he grabs it and runs, chewing it to bits and leaving pieces to puddle on the carpet.

His infatuation with water has existed since the day we brought him home. He jumps into the bathtub to drink out of the faucet. He tries to lap water from the kitchen faucet while I am washing dishes. He dips his head into the toilet for a drink. When the garden hose is running, he sticks his head under the nozzle to slurp.

The first time he saw a rotating lawn sprinkler he stood and observed its movements. Then he approached it, danced around behind it and then jumped into the stream to let it beat against his chest.

He also can't stand to see anything float in his water bowl.

Pieces of stray dog food, occasional lint and a wandering gnat or ant sometimes plop into his bowl. He spots it the moment he walks into the room, then bobs his nose in until he can catch it, either eating it or spitting it onto the tile floor.

I am considering hanging a sign in my kitchen doorway: "Enter with waders on."

Toy Names

Lying about on the floors and sofa in my home at any given time is an array of stuffed footballs, squeaky play things, knotted socks and tennis balls. This is the collection Speckles has gathered over the years.

Some of the balls my husband found on curbs while delivering newspapers. Those we sterilized and passed on to Speckles.

When I have a chance, usually when Speckles is outside, I pick up the toys in a hurry and toss them back into his toy box, a green plastic tub beside my sofa. That tub has now run out of room for toys.

The toys acquire names as time goes by, as Speckles sticks them in my face while I watch television or drops them in my lap while I am eating dinner. Speckles knows the name I have given to each toy, and if I tell him to get a specific one for me, he runs and finds it.

Plush toys take a beating from Speckles, but they are his favorites. He slobbers all over them, tosses them in the air, and eventually pulls their fur off with his front teeth.

His favorite toys are two stuffed footballs the size of real ones, a large stuffed moose, a squeaky green bird and a squeaky red toy soldier he received for Christmas from his golden Labrador friend, Chase.

The names of his toys are as follows:

Footsball – two stuffed footballs acquired from a local store for a couple dollars each. One I purchased, and the other came from my mom (whom we call his *grandmother*) for Christmas.

Moosel or Moose or Mooseltoe – his first toy since the age of three months. At first it was as big as Speckles, but now he lays his head on Moose and shakes it madly so its arms and legs box him about the head. My mom gave me Moose when I attended college. The animal now has been mended numerous times and is missing antlers, ears, his bottom lip and his tail hangs by a few threads.

Coo Coo Bird – a green squeaky bird with bulging yellow eyes. He received this toy from Chase for his first birthday.

Snakey – a plush toy for puppies. It looks like a pull toy with two loose ends, one containing a rattle and the other containing a squeaker.

Soldier – a red toy soldier that looks like a ball with a head. This toy he received from Chase for Christmas. The squeaker makes a very high-pitched, annoying sound.

Squeaky Football – we have a yellow one and an orange one, both from Chase. Speckles plays with these toys occasionally.

Hedgehog – we have two of these. One is blue and one is orange and both have knobby spines on their backs. These toys were intended as gifts for Chase, but Speckles didn't want to surrender them.

Bear Bear – a fuzzy bear-shaped toy with a squeaker in the middle. This also came from Chase for Christmas.

Whiffleball – two large Whiffleballs with holes in

them. I purchased these toys. Speckles showed interest in Whiffleballs after receiving one from my husband. He found one on a curb while delivering newspapers one morning. Speckles scoots the balls around the house with his nose, steps on them hard to make them fly into cabinets and bounce off walls. He growls, grunts, slams into furniture and basically has fun all by himself with the Whiffleballs.

Socky – old holey socks are knotted and passed on to Speckles. He has several white ones, a dark green one, and some black ones. They usually stay on the bottom of his toy bin until he sniffs them out and shakes them in front of my face.

Aside from these toys, we are always finding and cleaning up old baseballs, softballs, tennis balls, and Whiffleballs for Speckles. He keeps them in his toy bin and rummages his nose through the bin occasionally to find favorite playthings.

Traveling The Potty Trail

How many of you have horrible puppy potty-training tales to tell?

I have a few good ones to share.

At the age of ten months, Speckles had nearly perfected potty-time. Now he stands at the door whining, or runs to me, then runs back to the door and so on until I respond.

My husband and I tried a crate-training method when Speckles was a pup, thinking that the carpeting and furniture would remain spot-free. However, when we left him alone and ventured into another room or took a quick walk outside, he would invariably decide to *let it all go*.

Our one-year-old sofa became a comfort station. If I was in the kitchen doing dishes and Speckles had a sudden urge to tinkle, he would jump onto the cushions, stand with his front paws on the back of the structure and create a lovely zigzag pattern in yellow. More than once I spent an hour scrubbing down the fabric.

Our spare bed became his second comfort station. He would make these pit stops secretly, and I would only find them when I sat on the bed to change my clothes.

It took months to make him understand the word, "No." We thought he was defective internally –

lacking a complete bladder, blessed with short urinary tract tubes or just plain incontinent. Our veterinarian said that Speckles just didn't like to be alone, and that we needed to keep him in our sight at all times. If we couldn't do that, he needed to be placed in his crate.

His occasional tinkles and doodles wouldn't have bothered me if they were on the tile or the area rug by the front door. At least I would have known that he tried to make it outside. But Speckles preferred to use the sofa or the bed.

Several months passed, and we thought he had grown out of his potty training troubles. One night we thought he was mature enough to leave out of his crate while we slept.

My husband was supposed to take him outside in the middle of the night, but he didn't follow through. When I heard barking at 3 a.m., I rushed down the stairs and into the hallway barefooted.

Before I continue, I must say that when Speckles drinks, his flabby Brittany spaniel lips carry a lot of water with them into other parts of the house: basically, he dribbles.

When I stepped into the hallway and walked a little farther to find him, I realized that my feet were getting wet. Usually the trail of dribble ends several feet from the kitchen doorway, but that night, it didn't. I started flipping on lights in every room and discovered a zigzag trail of tinkle through the entire house. The sofa had also been used as a tree.

I bumbled around, absorbing liquid with paper towels and scrubbing down the trail. Then I locked Speckles in his crate.

This incident brought to light a new definition of anger. I was angry with my husband for not letting the dog outside, and I was angry at the dog for being stubborn.

Puppies are like toddlers, however. They have to learn where and when to potty. Some catch on fast. Others take their time. Speckles was just being a kid.

Trying To Find Peace

There aren't two moments of peace in my house when Speckles is loose.

If I sit down, he grabs something he shouldn't have and runs through the room chewing on it. I have to fling myself on him and snatch it away. I have recorded several items he has taken over the past two weeks. He always manages to seize stuff when I am unable to grab him quickly.

My nieces were playing checkers at my house one evening. When they were through with the game, the checkerboard and checkers were placed strategically in the middle of the dining room table so Speckles couldn't reach them.

That morning I had just started to put my nylons on, working them up to my knees, when I heard crunching nearby. Speckles came jogging into the room and spat out a checker on the floor. It no longer had a center, just the ring. Waddling through the house with my nylons at my knees, I grabbed him in the living room with two more checkers locked in his mouth.

One Friday I went to a grocery store and walked past him into the house with several bags of goodies. Speckles, knowing that each time I shop, I bring him home a rawhide bone, immediately ran for each sack, trying to find his bone. I dug through the sacks and pulled out my pack of gum and then placed the gum on the dining room table. After unpacking the groceries, I discovered my pack of gum on the floor with half of the sticks missing.

Feeling ambitious one afternoon, I made a vanilla/chocolate marble cake with chocolate frosting. I covered the cake with aluminum foil and put it on the stove. Foolishly, I went outside and left Speckles in the house alone. Later that night, when I went to eat a piece of my cake, the foil was mysteriously peeled back. Frosting was missing throughout the cake's midsection. A distinct tongue mark graced the edges.

After walking Speckles one afternoon, I returned home and brewed some fresh iced tea. Speckles received his ritual ice cube, and I sat my cool glass of tea on the dining room table. Then I walked across the room to grab a newspaper. On my way back I spotted him, front feet on the table's edge, lapping tea from the glass.

Every time I am in the kitchen cooking, he comes in to harass me. Out of the corner of my eye I will see a dog with no head. He sticks his head deep into the garbage can and sniffs around for empty cat food cans, meat wrappers and other leftover treats.

When it is time to fold laundry, he lies on the bed and steals socks from the baskets.

After the whole house is cleaned, sofa cushions are fluffed and in place, he pokes his nose behind the cushions, tossing them all onto the floor. Then he sits on them, panting with pride.

While I am watching television, he rubs along my plant stand and snips off bits of leaves in his mouth until I come after him.

People say children are a handful. When I tell mothers of young children about my dog's antics, they shake their heads in disbelief. Speckles is just like a child.

Tub Time

For all of the dog owners out there who have dealt with muddy paws after potty breaks on rainy days, this story is for you.

Speckles loves to romp through mud, dig in gardens and stand in the rain, no matter how hard the rain is coming down. Because of this, I try to wipe his paws with a hand towel when he comes in the back door. However, in time the mud splatters farther and farther up his legs, onto his belly, cakes around his nose and so on. A hand towel can't solve the problem and he will run through the house and jump onto the sofa, leaving muddy paw prints.

A friend of mine who owns two large dogs keeps baby wipes by her back door so she can wipe her pooches down when they come in from playing.

I decided to teach Speckles to run to the bathroom and jump into the bathtub so I could bathe his feet.

He likes to romp in a plastic kiddy pool in the summers, so I already knew he liked to stand in water.

Each time he comes in with muddy paws, I check him at the back door. We do an initial swabbing with a hand towel from his knees down. Before he enters the house farther, I tell him, "Get in the tub." He looks at me. I open a door to the kitchen, set him loose, and remind him, "Tub."

Speckles runs into the bathroom, jumps into the

tub and stands waiting for me. I kneel beside the tub in preparation.

I keep a small plastic bowl nearby and a spare washcloth and towel for these muddy situations. I turn on the water so it is lukewarm and fill the container. Each paw is dunked and swished. He raises each leg with my touch and allows me to rinse it. With the washcloth I swab his nose and cheeks. I run the wet cloth down his legs and scrub his chest. He stands and waits for me to finish. One day he even picked up a squeaky toy and put it in the tub to play with while I washed him.

Recently he's started to drink the water running into the drain after it washed over his paws. He stands and laps and laps until I stop him. Usually, by the time I am through, he has a full bladder again and has to go back out into the rain.

When we're finished with the foot washing I tell him, "Okay." He jumps from the tub and stands on the bathroom rug, waiting for me to dry his legs. Sometimes he licks his ankles while I rub them. He waits for me to open the bathroom door, and then he jogs out into the living room to play.

Several days ago, he decided to grab the foot-rinsing bowl from the bathroom and carry it around the house, bouncing it off of his nose and scooting it around on the kitchen tile floor. I thought it was cute until he started to chew the bowl along one edge and eat bits of plastic.

This foot-washing method works for me and guarantees clean toes every time. I also save my sofa cushions, blankets, and rugs from continuous spot cleanings. I think Speckles enjoys our footbaths too. He's accepting, and the water cools or warms his feet, depending on the weather outside.

Work Out

I've had quite a work out the last couple of days. Speckles has been learning to run outside for potty breaks without his leash on.

My husband can complete this task smoothly, quickly, without breaking a bead of sweat on his forehead. The dog also comes back looking rested, ears up and calmly meanders about the house.

I, however, am the one the dog waits for to take him outside. I am his buddy; I am the pushover. I am the one he either does not hear or simply chooses not to listen to.

Last night a neighbor girl was tossing rocks to him while he was chained in the front yard. I heard her saying to him, "Get the rocks!" "No, find the rocks!" Speckles just looked at her, ears up high and tongue drooping to his knees.

I observed their meaningless game for a moment and then went out to release him, sending him inside. I was barefoot, in boxer shorts and a T-shirt. The neighbor girl had gone home to play.

Normally when my husband releases Speckles to send him inside, he immediately shoots to the front door, bangs the door open with his front feet and darts inside for a treat. Last night, I was in control – or I thought I was.

When I unhooked his leash from the collar, tapped

him on the hind-end, and said, "Speckles, inside!", he took off running. He ran straight for the neighbor's house and around the side, trying to find the girl who threw rocks to him shortly before. I stood there shouting his name and then raced across the yard – barefoot.

Speckles kept running. I heard screaming and then a girl's voice shouting, "Leave me alone!" Speckles had found the girl, jumped up on her and was kissing her face.

He then dashed to the next neighbor's house. I spotted him under their porch. My feet were throbbing in pain, and rightly so, since I was walking through gravel with bare feet.

Speckles kept running. I looked up, and the neighbor's in-ground swimming pool came into view. From my left came the dog. Through the air went the dog. Into the water went the dog.

I was motionless for a brief moment, which seemed like eternity, trying to figure out how to get him out of the pool. He was paddling around in the eight-foot-deep end, ears floating on the water's surface. Then he became tangled in the safety rope lying on the water. I grabbed one of his legs, then another and hauled him onto dry land.

From there, I pulled him home by the collar.

This morning I didn't think he would try something like that again. I was wrong.

He took off to the neighbor's house, looked at the pool and then ran up the alley to a garage sale and began running around the tables of merchandise.

"Hi, Speckles!" I heard a neighbor lady say. He stopped to see her, and I nabbed him.

This time I was equipped with jogging shoes. I was

prepared for a long run. For now, Speckles will find himself daily *at the-end-of-his-rope*.

My Cats:

Desdemona,

Chocolate Drop,

Joan of Arc

and

Captain Jack Sparrow

Meeting Desdemona

My cats are quite possibly the best kinds of cats a person could own – strays.

Desdemona was from a family of four kittens. There were three girls and one boy born under my desk in college. Her mother, whom I named Daisy Mae, wandered around outside the college dorm for several days until I heard someone say that she might be pregnant.

When the shorthaired tabby came in out of the cold, I felt her large belly, confirming that she was expecting. I fed her, took her to a veterinarian, and was told that she was going to give birth within weeks. My efforts to place her through a humane society came to a halt. There was no room for an expectant mother and her babies.

Daisy and I grew to understand each other. She enjoyed the warmth of my bed comforter, and I made her a nesting box, lined with old towels, under my desk.

On an April day, I woke at 5 a.m. to the sound of tiny meows. I peeked into the box and saw she had four clean babies, two white and two black. She looked at me with relief, and I petted her head. Her babies were feeding quietly.

At the time, I was studying the works of William Shakespeare. Therefore, I named each baby after one of my favorite Shakespearean characters: Hamlet, Jessica, Ophelia, and Desdemona.

I held Desdemona the day she was born. She was the runt of the litter, but a feisty, talkative one. She had matter in her eyes and I lifted her carefully to clean them. Her mother watched every move. As the kittens matured, I showed them how to use a litter box, digging tiny holes in the litter with my finger while they nosed around. When they finished, I helped them cover their potties with their front paws.

When the kittens were too active for me to contain in a small dorm room, I brought them home to my parents. My parents had several cats of their own at the time, so I had to find a home for the new family.

I screened every possible response I received to a newspaper ad, and found only two people I trusted. One lady took Daisy and both black kittens. Ophelia, a white cat with one blue and one yellow eye, went to live with an elderly couple who kept in touch every year with photos of her.

Desdemona, I decided to keep. I always said I kept her because she was the smallest, but I know it was because she reminds me of her mother. Most importantly, we have uniquely communicated since the first day I held her, the day she was born.

Meeting Chocolate Drop
(C.D.)

A friend of mine in college owned Chocolate Drop. He got her from a friend who got her from a farm where she wasn't wanted any longer. We both decided to name her Chocolate Drop, or C.D. for short, because she is black and white with white feet, except for her black toes.

She was one or two months old, and a feisty girl, when she entered my life. She would scale the bunk beds, tear up paper, and chew on pencils. When my friend became a Resident Assistant on campus, he had to find another place to put her because animals weren't allowed. I secretly moved her into my dorm room temporarily – that is, until we found out if she would be accepted into my parents' or his parents' home.

C.D. became a mascot in my dorm. She sauntered into the lounge and chased me through rooms. Fellow cat lovers brought me cans of cat food on occasion. Many people asked me in the campus cafeteria how she was doing. She became my art study, and I filled pages in my sketchbook of her sleeping positions. She slept on my roommate's chest and drooled onto her face at night. She would lie on our desks while we studied and dip her paw into our water glasses unexpectedly.

During vacation breaks, my friend would pack her into an old wooden milk crate with a sliding lid and drive her to his home several hours away. Never once did she argue about the journey.

Then one day while I was studying in my dorm room, C.D. had a seizure. Initially, my roommate and I thought she was dying and we rushed her to a local veterinarian. I didn't care how much her veterinary care would cost, I asked the veterinarian to run tests to determine the cause of this seizure. The veterinarian guessed she had epilepsy. All of her blood tests were negative, so we lived day-to-day, wondering if the seizures would strike again.

They did recur, many months apart. We were told the seizures might disappear as she got older. If they became more frequent, she would need medication daily for the rest of her life. That would be expensive for two college students with little to no income. We needed to make a decision, my friend told me, to keep her or to put her to sleep.

I chose life.

As she aged, C.D.'s seizures began coming farther apart. Stressful situations, such as moving, seemed to aggravate her and encourage another seizure. I vowed to make her life calm and to provide her with the love she deserves. I believe that she is truly special; that is why I was given the chance to live with and learn from this creature with a devastating condition.

When a seizure strikes, I cover her with a towel or blanket until her trembling stops. I clean her if she soils herself and I talk softly to her, never leaving her side.

When a cat or dog with epilepsy comes out of a seizure, their pupils are dilated, and they seem confused. C.D. pushes herself up onto her feet and begins to talk to me in a soft, meowing tone. She walks around the house from room to room, reacquainting herself with the surroundings. The whole time, I follow her, talking to her in a gentle voice, reassuring her that I am with her. I do this because I know that I wouldn't want to be alone in her condition.

Because of all the times she met me at the door when I came home, watched me leave, sat on my lap when I am tired or sad, and lain beside me when I wrote or drew, I owe her my undivided attention.

I also learned there is only so much I can do for C.D. When she has a seizure, we cannot control her actions.

Three years passed between her seizures. Then a seizure came that hospitalized me for two days. She bit into my finger, locking her fangs. She hung on for several minutes until the muscles in her body relaxed. The result was an infection in my tendon, and I needed to be placed on intravenous antibiotics.

Still, C.D. remains loyal to me and trusts me more than any other human she knows. After every seizure, she returns to her loving, purring, drooling self, and I treasure the times we spend together.

Meeting Joan of Arc

Joan of Arc presented herself to me while I was driving home one evening. I saw two lumps in the road and straddled them with my car tires. When I passed over them, I noticed one lump looking up at me with wide, terrified eyes. I stopped instantly and jumped out to save her.

Joan's sibling was deceased, hit by another car, and I laid it on the curb. Joan, however, hissed at me with all her 1-pound might. I tucked her into my coat and rushed her home.

I was concerned that my dog would mistake her for a squirrel and try to chase her, but Joan stood her ground. She sat in the middle of my bed and allowed me to comb her. She was covered with gray paint that had to be cut away. Speckles and his sisters watched me diligently, sniffing Joan's face.

After her brushing, Joan walked around my bedroom and I noticed her limping on one back leg. A local veterinarian diagnosed her with a broken toe.

I considered adopting Joan to a loving home, but I

couldn't. I named her Joan of Arc because of her determination and strength to live through anything. She's headstrong and stands up to my sixty-pound Brittany spaniel. She jumps on the backs of her sisters and rides them through the house, making them hiss all the way. With me, she stands on countertops and puts her front feet on my chest, flirting for affection. She's my little Joanie, my little "J-Bird," my little "J."

Meeting
Captain Jack Sparrow

Jack is mentioned just a few times in this book since he is the latest addition to the family. I know he will grace many more stories in the future.

My friend, Jo, lived in a three-story home next door to a funeral parlor in the heart of our city. The street in front of her house consists of four lanes of traffic and is very busy. Jo always seemed to have stray cats show up at her back door. Most were females who brought their babies, or females who were very pregnant. Jo, being a cat lover, tried to take them all in and have them spayed/neutered at her own expense. She spent a great deal of money helping strays receive veterinary care and finding them new homes.

Unfortunately, Jo and her husband decided to move out West, and she had to find homes for several cats still in her possession. A new mother had just brought several kittens to her house, too.

I stopped by Jo's home one afternoon and looked

at several kittens still running around her backyard. Jo had not been able to catch them all yet.

Traffic was whizzing in front of her home, and all the kittens scurried for shelter when they saw me outside with Jo – except for one black-and-white kitten that remained seated under a bush next to the funeral home. This little kitten was fixated on a bunch of sparrows sitting in the bush above it. The kitten's eyes were huge, and it didn't move when we tried to call it to us.

I told Jo that day, "That's a cutie pie." I already had two black-and-white adult cats at home.

A day or two later, Jo called me and asked me to come over to her house. She told me in a phone message, "I have your kitten." She was able to grab all of the kittens as they came to her back door to eat.

I went by her house to see the kittens, thinking that Jo was planning on giving them all to a local shelter so they could find homes.

Jo had the kitten, a male, in a crate by himself along with a stuffed toy resembling a black-and-white killer whale. When she opened the crate, the kitten came out and jumped into my arms to rest. He acted as though I was his. I couldn't say, "No" to Jo.

I initially named the little man Sparrow after the sparrows he was infatuated with. I received Sparrow shortly after I lost my job and my life was in a whirlwind. Shamans say that sparrows are spirit messengers that teach us how to *find your soul song*. I found that message fitting for the time Sparrow came into my life.

Sparrow was three months old when I brought him home in January, so I planned to celebrate his birthday on my birthday, October 4. He was my first male cat.

Eventually, Sparrow's name evolved into Captain Jack Sparrow after the lead character in the movie, Pirates of the Caribbean. Actor Johnny Depp played Captain Jack Sparrow. He was a handsome pirate – a ladies' man who was always drunk on rum. So my little Sparrow became Jack Sparrow.

Jack had really big ears and a little head when he was a youngster. I always joked that he would one day *grow into his ears*. And he did. Jack evolved from just a couple of pounds to a muscle-bound, long-legged, long-bodied, and eighteen-pound feline by the age of six.

Catnip

One thing my mom has always grown in her garden, mainly for her cats, is catnip.

My brother and I used to pick leaves off of the plants and bring them in the house and watch her cats go bonkers, meowing and following us, rolling around on the floor, drooling excessively and eventually boxing each other about the head.

Catnip has that effect on felines. They eat it like candy and then act as if they just drank a bottle of alcohol.

My neighbor had one stray stalk of catnip pop up along her fence. My two fat cats, C.D. and Desdemona, decided to chew it to the ground one afternoon while they were romping around in our backyard. Their pupils dilated, their ears twitched and they scampered like racehorses about the yard.

My mom still has several cats and grows even more catnip plants in her garden. My brother still brings each of the cats a chunk of catnip, waves it in front of their faces, and then leads them like the Pied Piper through the house. Once they are all gathered in one room, he lays the pieces on the floor, and we watch the cats eat and roll ecstatically. When they start wrestling each other, we intervene.

A friend of mine claims she has a box of the most potent catnip shavings around. She keeps it in her refrigerator, in a plastic bag, because her cats sniff it out anywhere else she puts it. Occasionally she brings the box out and leads her cats to the living room, where she sprinkles the catnip on the rug. Immediately, they all start rolling around.

One time I visited, she decided to sprinkle the catnip on the cats too. That turned the room into a war zone.

When I was a child, my mom and I would buy our cats each a catnip toy for Christmas, wrap the toys and let each cat tear theirs open on Christmas day. I remember a cat-mat, a fabric toy stuffed with batting and catnip shavings, that one of our cats took possession of, slobbered on until it was soaked and then tore to shreds. The twenty-dollar mat, once we restrained the cat and got it away, was quickly disposed of.

Those little batta-toys, catnip-stuffed birds and fish on elastic strings, never last around my cats. They chew the strings off and run away with their catnip catch.

Last year I was making catnip mice for a local animal foundation fund-raiser, and my two cats decided to watch. When I wasn't shooing them away, they were creeping closer to me on their bellies, then sticking their heads into my sewing bag and sniffing like bloodhounds.

If you are a cat owner and have never experienced a cat's behavior after they eat this intoxicating herb, you should try it. Catnip is guaranteed to get even the fattest or oldest of cats into a playful mood, even if the mood is just a slight bit of rolling or batting of their paw.

Closet Searcher

Every evening when I come home from work, one of my lower kitchen cupboard doors is standing open. I close it, turn away for a while and come back to find it standing open again.

This mysterious cupboard door opening happens every day.

At first, I wondered if my house was haunted. But in reality, the ghost was and still is my white cat, Desdemona.

I watched her one afternoon as she sat on the kitchen floor. She casually opened the cupboard door by placing the claws of her left front foot behind the edge of the door and swinging it open wide into the room.

She looked around inside of the cabinet, and then walked away, leaving my pots and pans on display.

I should have known the surreptitious door opener was Desdemona. She has been a *closet searcher* for years, and a persistent one too.

Every morning she sits on my bed beside my head, staring at my face, waiting for my eyes to blink, then she starts biting my fingers until I get up and feed her.

While I get dressed for work and wander from the bathroom to the bedroom, she follows me, trying to get my attention by pawing at closet and cabinet doors. She doesn't stop until I open them all.

I already leave one closet door open for her; this is where she takes shelter during thunderstorms.

In the bathroom, she pulls at the sink cupboard door while I am standing in front of it. Her persistent thumping of the door annoys me until I let her inside the cupboard.

No matter what cupboard or closet she goes into, she only circles it once and comes back out.

"What is the purpose of this?" I often ask her.

She looks at me, rubs against my leg and moves on to closets in another room.

Maybe she thinks forbidden zones should be open twenty-four hours. Maybe she thinks something exciting is in there. Maybe she just likes to keep me active by following her around.

Whatever the case may be, anyone who visits my house will find my cupboard and closet doors standing open. Nothing is private here.

Paper Wads

It is amazing the entertainment a simple paper wad will provide for my cats.

They especially love the little note-cube-size paper wads; these fit just right in their little mouths.

From rooms away, they can hear me tear and crumple paper, and they run top-speed, *chirping* (as I call their little meows) into the room.

My cats, Desdemona and C.D., have always loved paper wads. Bouncy rubber balls, they turn their heads away from. String keeps their attention only if you keep wiggling it. A paper wad they can bat around and play with for hours.

Desdemona, who I think is a gifted kitty, learned to fetch paper wads and retrieve them. She especially loves it when I throw the wads onto a tile surface so she can run, slide into things, and come skidding back to me with her treasure.

The whole way, she talks in her little meowing fashion. When she comes back to me, she spits out the wad in front of me and then lies down and waits for another round of running.

The house I used to live in had carpeting throughout. She enjoyed it when I tossed one of the paper wads through an open railing upstairs. It bounced down the steps and she flung herself over the side, falling several steps down to get it. After a few seconds of rapid thumping, I heard her meow, and then her feet pitter-pattered back up the stairs. She carried the wad carefully between her front teeth.

Several trips later, her blood pressure rose, and her white fur accentuated her cherry-red nose and pink ears.

My other cat, C.D., has learned to catch the wads. She sits bobbing her head like a dove. I toss a wad towards her, and she clasps it in the air between her soft paws. Once she has it, she brings it to her mouth and then puts it on the floor.

When my cats lived at my mom's house, we would find stashes of paper wads under low-sitting objects such as chairs, the humidifier, and the refrigerator. Once the stashes were uncovered, the cats would come and inspect their reserves, sniffing each paper wad.

Paper wad time is a sacred occasion between my cats and me. We lay on the floor together, bat the wads back and forth, and I rapidly ruffle up their fur with my hands.

My dog, Speckles, has decided he should be in on the paper-wad action, too. When Desdemona least expects it, he dashes in and swoops the wads away in his slobbering mouth. The problem is, he doesn't bring them back. He lies in a corner and shreds them, eating them piece-by-piece.

Potty Training

From across the house the plastic liner rustles. In come little paws thumping across the floor.

It is ritual litter box cleaning time. As cat lovers know, when this takes place, every cat in the house comes running to watch. They sit in corners several feet away, or up on cabinets and sink tops, glaring.

As soon as the box is back in position, they are in it, making their marks.

There are only three things I can think of that get my two cats into the same room quickly and without fighting – litter-box cleaning, the can opener running and the smell of catnip.

C.D. often has me on my knees cleaning the kitchen floor. She doesn't like to walk in dirty litter, even if it has only one potty in the litter box. So, she tiptoes into the box, arches her back, squats a tad bit and projectile pees over the side. I tried a litter box with a lid to retain her fluids, but she stepped just inside of the doorway and peed right onto the floor.

I have tried using shredded newspaper, a little less litter, different types of litter and so forth. Still, she aims over the side.

To make matters worse, she tries to cover up her mini-lakes, tiptoeing back out of the litter box and scooping litter out onto the floor. She even attempts to rake the tile over it, to no avail.

Occasionally, I catch her walking into the box, and I push her fanny down to the litter, praising her while she is doing her duty. When she's through, she hops out, kicking her feet and flinging scoopable litter all over the floor. This, of course, feels very soothing on my bare feet.

There are several types of litter-box artists cat owners can identify with.

There are the cats that just can't find the right spot when they go. They dig here, turn, dig there, turn, dig a little deeper, turn ….

There are the mountain makers. They go potty and then move the entire contents of the litter box over the one tiny area they used.

There are the wall scrapers and paper shredders, who stroke with their paws until they are exhausted.

And, of course, there are those who don't cover it up at all. Those of us with fragranced candles or air fresheners nearby know who those furry felines are.

In C.D.'s situation, I often wonder what it would be like if she had to go potty outside. Would she still dig in one spot and aim her stream over the hole?

Maybe her habits are linked to her upbringing. I acquired C.D. as a kitten while I was a sophomore in college. I harbored her in my dorm room with a litter box under my desk. I plunked her into it several times to show her where to go. She never peed over the side then.

Desdemona was born under my desk during my junior year of college. Her mom was found wandering around campus. I took her in and found out that she was due to have kittens in several days. Thus, Desdemona and three other kittens came along.

I held Desdemona the day she was born. When

she was old enough to start potty training, I dug little holes for her in the litter box with her front paws. Then I positioned her just right over the hole so she could go potty.

The litter box is a sacred place for cats, I think. Some cats don't mind an audience while they are going. Others will potty quickly and run away if they know someone is watching.

I think people are like this, too. Some of us can squat in the woods, others are too embarrassed or disgusted to use public restrooms, and most all of us enjoy a relaxing time in our own restroom behind closed doors.

Survivor

Since she has entered my life, Joan suffered multiple mishaps that, if they happened to a child, would have been grounds to alert the Department of Children and Family Services.

Her history is one filled with adventure and survival.

Found at 9 p.m. on a city street, Joan was a mere one-pound. A sibling was with her, but deceased from being hit by a car.

I picked Joan up and rushed her home, placing her sibling on the curb before we departed. A man nearby said he would bury the little one's body. Joan was splattered with gray paint and shaking with fear.

She endured intense grooming by me while nestled on my bed. When we were through, she was minus whiskers on one side – a result of paint that needed to be cut away from her fur.

Four pounds and several months later, those same whiskers were eliminated again by coming too close to a burning candle.

Aside from hitting her head against the bathroom sink while in mid-jump from the bathtub, she has survived the following:

    * singeing fur on her left side and losing all whiskers on the left side during an encounter with a

tea-light candle. This took place while I was taking a shower one night. I exited my bathroom to smell burnt fur and searched for the victim. Joan had leaped from the floor to the top of a small television where the candle was burning.

* being soaked in the shower. "Now you see her, now you don't" is the game Joan plays while I take showers. Alone one minute, I can turn around the next minute to find her furry black mass observing me from behind.

* swaying two stories up in a pine tree. Joan enjoys garden romps with me, under supervision.

On one particular evening she scaled my chain link fence and climbed up a pine tree nearby. The closer I came to touching her, the higher she climbed. Before long, she was higher than my house.

I thought that spraying her with a garden hose would scare her down. However, it soaked her and sent her higher. She began to cry.

Three hours after calling her name, scaling ladders as high as possible and trying the lure of cat food, rain started to fall.

Joan was crying louder.

Wind started to blow.

I called for assistance from my amateur tree-climbing brother.

With a tall ladder and large pruning shears, he removed several branches, helping him come into arm's reach of the little five-pound, shivering feline.

A week later, I was still cutting pinesap-clustered hairballs from her tummy fur.

What will Joan's next escapade be? I don't look

forward to finding out. Her full name suits her personality – Joan of Arc, a heroine.

Teaching Desdemona Ballet

Desdemona did a graceful ballet move last night that I am proud of. The landing, however, needs some work.

Every night when I shower, I leave the bathroom door open a crack for her to come in. If I don't – all you cat lovers out there can attest to this – she will hear the door shut and come running from rooms away to scratch quietly at the bottom of the door until I let her in. She thinks I am having too much fun behind closed doors, and she wants to be included.

Because I have a dog three times her size, she likes having the door open before she comes scratching. This way, when Speckles comes running after her down the hall, she can dart inside. The bathroom floor plan doesn't make this quick movement on her part very easy.

The door swings open in front of the toilet next to the sink and is immediately followed by a tub along the back wall. Desdemona usually shoots through the crack and behind the toilet into the main room. Or she flies up on the toilet seat and then onto the sink.

Sometimes the toilet seat is up and she straddles the seat across the water on the approach to the sink.

She has learned now that smooth ceramic or plastic does not mix with furry paws.

Last night I took my eyeglasses off and laid them

on the corner of the sink near the toilet. My husband had just taken the dog outside for a late night potty break, so Desdemona decided she'd just sit and look at me through the doorway. She started to doze off before the dog came back in. This allowed him to get a head start in running down the hall after her.

While I stood there, blind without my glasses, in through the doorway shot a white streak, the door flew open, I leaned closer to get a look and only saw dilated pupils and pink ears. Desdemona's toes gripped the edge of the sink. I heard my glasses fall into the sink and then a splash.

Desdemona had fallen into the toilet.

The dog took off running back down the hall – mission accomplished.

Desdemona sat in the bathroom licking her hindquarters, shaking each foot, and giving me a shower with toilet water.

Desdemona has never been too graceful. Although, her flowing, long white hair and wide, yellow eyes make up for her lack of grace.

When she walks, her hind legs are bowed at the knees and she swings her feet outward.

You'd think she'd learn her lesson about furry paws and slick surfaces. Quite often she has leaped up onto the dining room table and slid right off the other side into the wall.

When she was living at my mom's house during my college days, Desdemona decided to climb down the side of the house from the roof one afternoon. My mom lets her cats out on the roof, which is fairly flat, to get fresh air. Normally, they do not jump off; they just watch birds fly overhead and let the breeze blow through their fur.

To climb down the side of the house, Desdemona used ivy attached to the siding as her ladder. Once she got to the ground, she was petrified and tried to get back into the house.

Instead of walking around the house to a door, she decided to leap up onto the side of the house in an attempt to climb back to the roof. My mom found Desdemona flinging herself against the siding and brought her back inside.

The Smartest Cat on Earth

I call my cat C.D. "The Smartest Cat on Earth."

Sure, her sister Desdemona is intelligent, but C.D. has done some remarkably funny, ingenious things over the past few years. Many of those things happened only this past summer.

Very seldom has C.D. wanted to eat table scraps. She grew up with me in a college dorm room for about one year, and then lived with my parents until I was out of school.

Students in college would try to entice her with tidbits of hamburger or macaroni and cheese, but C.D. didn't care about those goodies. She only wanted to her canned food or little kitty food crunchies.

As far as sweets go, she will lick a little ice cream from my fingertip or a little whipped topping here and there. To my surprise, one day I found her indulging in a secret fetish.

I was heading back to work from lunch one afternoon and saw her sitting on my dining room table next to a glass candy dish. She was bending over, then she lifted her head slowly to look at me, then her head went back down.

In the candy dish were malted milk balls, and she was gently licking the chocolate with the tip of her tongue. Knowing that chocolate can be harmful to pets, I immediately took the dish of candy away. She gave me a puzzled look and continued to lick her lips.

When it comes to getting my attention, C.D. finds me in unusual places at unusual times.

Some mothers of children say that when they use the bathroom at home, they always have their children or husband calling after them through the door once it is closed.

I've learned with my cats and dog to leave the bathroom door slightly ajar, or to wait for them to enter the bathroom with me before I shut the door. It never fails; the cats always dart from under a table or out of a window to be with me while I am in the bathroom.

Recently, C.D. has taken up tightrope walking while I am going to the bathroom. She jumps up onto the edge of the bathtub and tiptoes along it to where she can stand and stare at me while I am occupied. Now she ventures farther and reaches out to me, placing her front paws on my legs and moving just a wee bit closer until she can try to lie down on my lap.

Watching her turn around on the bathtub edge is quite entertaining. Occasionally she slips, but she doesn't mind sitting in the tub if she falls. She used to sit in the tub and stare at the faucet, waiting for drops of water to fall.

Once she stood in the bathtub and looked at a trickling stream until her ears and whiskers were covered with mist. Then I had to shut the water off, blot her face dry, and pull her out of the tub.

She also likes to chase little wads of toilet paper that I toss into the tub for her. I only wish I could teach her to pick them up after playtime. I have found many soggy toilet tissue balls floating around my ankles while showering.

Recently she figured out a way to escape my fenced-in back yard – quickly and secretly. She knows I will hunt her down, so her desire to leave has become a game between us.

When I notice she is missing, I leave the yard, call her name, and she darts back to the spot under the fence whence she escaped. I watched her one afternoon as she squeezed her body through a gap under the fence gate. It is amazing how her twelve-pound body can fit through a five or six-inch gap between the ground and the chain link.

Now, however, she has learned that the more weedy and bushy the area she hides in, the longer it will take for me to find her and pull her out. She slithers under my neighbor's grapevines, hides under his pine trees and under his boat, sitting on the trailer. It once took a long stick and a poke in her rear end with it to get her off of the boat trailer.

Her latest hide-away retreat is a covered bird feeder sitting on a fire pit in my yard.

I lost track of C.D. one afternoon, and I heard birds hollering. I searched the ground, bushes, looked outside of the yard and came back to find her sitting in the bird feeder. Her tail was hanging out of one end, flipping back and forth gently. She looked at me with sleepy eyes and sat there peacefully, basking in the sun's rays. I patted her on the head, shook my head, and grabbed a camera from inside of the house to capture this moment.

Birds still swoop down to feed at this feeder, but they shriek when they find C.D.'s black-and-white fur sticking out of the sides. She knows she can't get any closer than this to her feathered friends. Every time she goes outside with me now, the feeder is the first place she heads for.

The "Twitchies"

Occasionally, when my cats are in a playful mood, we sit on the floor together and play with things, such as socks, pillow cases, paper wads or plastic milk jug rings.

I try to mimic their actions, or, as I call them, their *twitchies*. Cat owners probably know what I am talking about. It is when a cat gets quarter-size eyes, squats down to the floor, and wiggles his rump back and forth, ready to pounce on something.

Desdemona is the twitchy queen. She gets the twitchies whether she is playing inside or rolling around outside in the dirt while I am gardening.

Each night I crumple up paper wads before I go to bed. The cats run to my office and watch me wad them up tight. Then they follow me into the dining room, where I toss the paper wads into the kitchen on the tile floor.

Desdemona leaps first, sliding across the tile, meowing all the way. She tries to stop when she gets to an area rug, but slides a few feet farther and crashes into a piece of furniture.

C.D. hasn't mastered the art of sliding like her sister. She coasts a few inches, then tiptoes the rest of the way.

Desdemona always returns the paper wads to me for another run through the kitchen. One night she slid into the kitchen cabinet several times head first, before she realized that what she was doing hurt.

Socks and pillowcases are fun to toss on top of their backs. They run several feet until the sock or pillowcase slips down to the tail and onto the floor. I wave the objects in front of their faces, and they jump and swat at every movement.

Twitchies ruled the other night, when I was decorating a sheet to be used as a backdrop for a fund-raising photography event for a local humane organization.

My girls decided to ride on the sheet through the house as I dragged it behind me to the living room. C.D. didn't realize she could actually ride the sheet; instead, she used it as a treadmill, walking her stubby legs as fast as she could on the sheet, getting nowhere fast.

Both of them enjoy it when I wiggle my hands and feet under blankets in bed. They jump and pounce at every movement, flipping off the bed and back on.

Desdemona likes to run after me, drop to the floor on her side and play dead so I will get on the floor with her, rub her fur the opposite way, roughing her up gently but quickly. She pretends to want to get away, dodges off under a chair, and then comes back for more.

The cats' behavior during playtime always makes me laugh. Desdemona's blood pressure rises and her pink nose and ears turn a deeper shade of red. C.D.'s tail curls over at the tip and stands straight as a flagpole. She runs away from me and sits under a dining room chair, thinking I can't see or touch her. They talk to me in little chirping meows, opening their mouths slightly. I talk back to them softly, with little *tsk tsk* noises.

When they are finished playing, they lie on the floor to rest. I touch their heads lightly and scratch one ear. They accept my soothing touch and a kiss on the head.

Valuable Lessons

Some valuable lessons my kitten, Joan, has learned:

- It is easy to slide into the bathtub, but not as easy to get back out.
- Birdbaths have water in them.
- I can bite the dog's cheeks and ankles, but not Mommy's.
- Ear lobes are not nipples.
- My nose fits well into Mommy's nostrils.
- Frosted Flakes and milk are to me like cake and ice cream are to Mommy.
- My back legs can propel me faster than the front ones.
- A tail is a fascinating appendage.
- Drops of water from the bathroom faucet are never dull to watch.
- I can chew on Mommy's fuzzy slippers, but not her toes.
- Legs are not tree trunks.
- Ants will grab on to your nose if you sniff them.
- Hair makes good nesting material.

Adventures
of
All My Furry Children

Answering Machine Messages

I came home one afternoon and spotted my answering machine message light flashing. I asked Speckles who had called.

When the message played, I found out it was my husband, Brad, calling to see how I was doing. He had been seven hundred fifty miles away on business for over three weeks, and Speckles and I hadn't seen him since. Speckles stood near the machine, listening.

At the end of the message, Brad started addressing the dog and our cats, Desi and C.D., in a childish manner.

"Deeter" (that's one of C.D.'s nicknames), get out from under the bed and have a social life. Desdemona, stop purring and drooling in front of Speckles' cage. Speckles, tell Mommy I'm kinda looking for her."

I laughed while the words played, and Speckles stood in the doorway to the kitchen looking at the back door. His head tilted from left to right, thinking that my husband was actually in the house talking to him.

About a week later, my mom called and left an answering machine message. This time, she started off the conversation with Speckles instead of me.

"Speckles! Speckles! What are you doing Speckles?"

My family members aren't the only ones who leave answering machine messages for their pets.

The American Animal Hospital Association took a survey and learned that thirty-three percent of those who responded talk to their dogs through the phone or answering machine.

I have friends who have put their pets' voices on answering machine tapes too.

A cat referred to as Rotundo because of her large figure, left a short, familiar message for callers at a friend's house. At the end of the owner's message, the cat gave an irritating cry. It sort of sounded like the owner squeezed her to get the creature to speak.

I also have tried to get my cat, Desi, to speak on command into the answering machine, but failed. She stopped talking just when I had the tape ready.

However, I have captured Speckles grunting and panting and shaking his rattle toys.

If I could only get the cats or dog to answer the phone when it rings, then I would have it made.

My mom has several cats that have knocked her phone off of the receiver when it rings. My dad called home once and someone picked up the phone but didn't speak. The next few times he called, the line was busy. My dad was stranded at work because he couldn't reach my mom for a ride home.

We later watched one of her cats paw at the ringing phone until he knocked it off of the base. The case of the silent phone answerer was solved.

Attention Getters

It seems that pets will get your attention in any way possible. My pets are masters of the art, especially when I find precious time for myself.

There are the feline pencil-biting bouts while I am writing letters or filling out checks.

Then there is Speckles wedging stuffed animals between my knees from behind while I am standing.

If I ignore Speckles, he searches the house for anything to clench in his teeth: used tissues, socks, slippers, and cat toys.

I witnessed a wrestling match between sixty-pound Speckles, and his new feline sister, Joan, five-pounds.

I was sitting at my dining room table writing checks when I heard a thumping noise coming repeatedly from a wall behind me.

I called their names, "Speckles. Joan. What are you doing in there?"

They ignored me; the thumping became louder, now with an occasional grunt or *meow* interspersed.

Again, I dropped what I was doing and went to inspect their ruckus.

A shoe flew out of my closet in front of me.

"What are you doing?" I asked.

They were both in my closet with the door partly shut. My clothes were pulled off of hangers, shoes were out of boxes, Joan was in one corner, and

Speckles' head was buried under a dress.

"Okay. Everybody out of the closet!" I told them.

They scurried out of the wrestling ring – Joan hiding under my bed, Speckles running to the living room.

Bonding

When I first introduced my cats to my dog, I was afraid they would never get along.

Desdemona and C.D., ages five and seven, were used to living with my mom's small terrier named Sugar. Sugar thought that she was a cat, cleaning her face with strokes of her forelegs, licking the cats and wrestling with them. The cats, in turn, weren't afraid of her. They often attacked her playfully from behind when she wasn't looking, or jumped on top of her while she was sleeping.

After I moved Desdemona and C.D. to my house, we got Speckles, the Brittany spaniel. As Speckles grew, the cats couldn't control him. Since Speckles doesn't have another dog to play with, he wants to play with the cats.

I remember shortly after the dog moved in with us, one evening he came walking up to me with one of the cat's claw sheaths stuck in the top of his nose. I knew he had met with opposition.

Several days later, I heard a yelp from upstairs, where C.D. usually hides under our bed. When I ran up to save him, Speckles nosed in my arms playfully. When I looked at my arms, they were covered in blood. C.D. had caught Speckles' tender ear on an upswing and caused a cut. I rushed him to the bathtub where I washed his wound.

Today, the cat and dog relationships in my house have changed. Several times I have watched Desdemona roll playfully on the floor, practically begging the dog to pounce on her. He has learned to fear the cats' claws, so he keeps his distance.

When Speckles goes upstairs, he knows C.D. will be lying under the bed. He slithers around the perimeter of the room, and then leaps several feet to the mattress. Many times I have heard him whining up there. He gets on the opposite side of the room and fears coming back around because C.D. might shuffle out like a crab and grab him.

Once she did go after him, tail and back arched and bouncing towards him. Speckles' back legs move faster than his front legs, and he runs into walls trying to get away.

Desdemona, however, doesn't make him tremble. When she least expects it, Speckles runs up behind her and gooses her with his wet nose. She no longer runs from him; she simply saunters from room to room, looking casually back at him to monitor his actions. She has an outgoing, non-fearing personality.

When I hear her meow in disgust, a high-pitched, long drawl, I know I need to intervene.

As Speckles and my cats bonded more closely, I felt better about their future relationship. I could leave them alone in the house together without the fear of them being shaken like stuffed toys.

C.D., finally, after seven months, comes downstairs while Speckles is in the room. She allows him to sniff her face, her eyes grow wide, and then she beats him about the head until he departs.

Quite frankly, I think Desdemona is just plain tired of Speckles harassing her.

One day while I was washing dishes, I heard him snorting behind me. Desdemona had been sunbathing moments before. I turned around quietly and watched them. Speckles put one of Desdemona's ears in his mouth, like a lollipop, and gently pulled from base to tip. She just rested there, shaking her head. Then she rolled casually on the rug. His head tilted from left to right.

At night, when Speckles goes to bed in his crate, Desdemona creeps up to the crate door and peeks at him through the bars.

She is his buddy, his partner in crime. While he sits between my husband and me at the dinner table, waiting for handouts, Desdemona sits on the other side of me, waiting for hers. When he gets a bite, she gets a bite.

They have definitely bonded.

Clipping Nails, Combing Fur

I've gotten the procedure down to a science now when it comes time to clip Speckles' toenails.

When it is time to comb him and my two cats, the procedure is also a routine.

During nail clipping time, I sit on the floor in the living room and Speckles approaches me slowly. I put one arm around his neck and he lowers himself to his belly on the floor in front of me.

To stabilize his movements, I have to straddle his back and place one of my legs on his top back leg so it doesn't twitch. I hold a front paw in my hands and try to hold his head down with my left elbow.

All the while, he gently chews on my free hand, wrist, and the toenail clippers.

Throughout the process, I say, "No bite," and "Easy," and "Do you want a treat?"

He fights harder when I clip his front toenails than when I clip his back ones, which I can clip rather quickly.

Holding all sixty-pounds of Speckles still so I do not clip the nails too closely is definitely a challenge. He weighs nearly half as much as I do.

We also have a routine when it comes to cleaning his ears.

Speckles develops yeast infections in his ears from time to time. I try to keep his ears in good health by looking into them and cleaning them out with gauze and cotton swabs, then applying medicine from our veterinarian.

When I go to the bathroom closet and take out a gauze box, Speckles knows what is going to happen. Since his ears are tender when they are infected, I take extra care when cleaning residue from the folds of his outer ear.

He lies on his side, and I place half of my body over him while working. When the cleaning is done and the ointment is in, I rub the side of his head gently where his ear canal runs. Sometimes he grunts softly and I tell him, "It's okay."

In the top left drawer of my bedroom dresser I keep a red-handled comb with tight, black teeth. Anytime I open that drawer and pull out the comb, both of my cats come running to greet me. I sometimes run my finger along the teeth of the comb to make them clink together, a sound the cats love to hear.

For Desdemona, combing time is like being licked from head to toe by her mother. She rolls and drools and touches my hand with her paw for more.

C.D. used to become agitated when I combed her. She would walk past me for another stroke of the comb down her back, but when she felt the comb pull her hair, she would attack the first animal to come near her – usually poor, unsuspecting Speckles.

Today, C.D. enjoys being combed when we are alone in a room or outside in the garden. She walks away and comes back to me routinely for another stroke of her fur. Her haunches and tail are two areas she does not like me to comb, but a good chin-hair fluffing and cheek rubbing make her purr with contentment.

Both of my cats watch the clumps of fur I gather from their coats as if they are taking inventory of how much fur they are losing.

Speckles likes to be combed while he is looking out a picture window in my living room. He sits on a padded cedar chest and watches squirrels and people pass by while I run the comb down his back, over his haunches, through his long spaniel ear hair and through the curly hairs on his cropped tail.

Convenience

Folding laundry one day while standing in my living room, I realized yet another way to describe my dog and cats – convenient.

That afternoon I was folding towels. Speckles stopped beside me, bumped against my leg, and decided to wait for a pat on his back. Instead, I laid my towel on his back and used his sturdy frame as a clothes-folding stand. He stood and waited for me to fold my towel before he ran around the room, chasing his squeaky toys.

He is also convenient in other ways. He is a pillow when he sits beside me on the sofa and I place my head against his neck. He lies at my feet and I burrow my cold toes into his hair for warmth.

If I accidentally drop pieces of food, such as broccoli or breadcrumbs, on the floor while cooking, he licks them up immediately.

When I am gardening, he carries sticks to the compost pile for me. When I am digging holes to plant flower bulbs, he helps me dig.

Occasionally he brings clean laundry to me from baskets full of items waiting to be folded. Though he means well by bringing me a pair of my underwear, because he shakes them wildly in his slobbery mouth, I generally have to wash them again.

Desdemona and C.D. are my mini masseuses. I lie

on my stomach on my bed and they take turns climbing on top of me, massaging my lower back and shoulders.

All of my furry kids are bug catchers. Some bugs are more appealing to them than others, like a black ant on my back entry steps that caught Desdemona's eye one evening.

The irony of this delicate-looking white, pink-eared cat licking a large black ant from the steps made me first gasp with disgust, then laugh with disbelief as she casually walked away after the insect was consumed.

Speckles has found that bees buzzing around blooming bachelor buttons in my backyard are fascinating. He stands and waits for them to come near me when I am gardening, then he leaps and bites at the ones invading my space.

I must credit all of my furry kids with helping me keep in shape. When I am not bending over and cleaning the litter box and food dishes, scrubbing floors and wiping off Speckles' muddy paws, I am running with them through the house or the backyard.

I throw a ball across the yard and Speckles runs after it. While he is running after the ball, I hide behind a tree. When he spots me, I run away, with him following in hot pursuit.

At night, I throw mini paper wads through the house and onto the tile kitchen floor. Desdemona slides across the floor on the kitchen rug after the first one, slamming into the cupboard. C.D. follows Desi's technique when I throw the next wad of paper. Once they are in the kitchen, I hide behind the doorway and wait for them to come find me. When they walk around the doorway, I make a noise and scare them back into the kitchen.

Sometimes I run from them, and they chase me from room to room.

Most importantly, my pets are listeners, observers and counselors, lying on my lap when I am upset or tired, and jumping about happily when I am full of energy. I talk to them, and they look into my eyes with simple understanding.

Doing Chores

The pet care chores start each morning in my house, usually around 6:30. The alarm chimes. Desdemona is sitting beside my head on my pillow. She looks at me. Meows. Then, paws at my hands or face.

It's breakfast time, and Desi makes sure I am annoyed enough to rise and feed her.

C.D. sits on the floor beside the bed making sure Desi is successful in making me move.

From the living room, I hear Speckles whining from his crate. I rise from the bed and lift window shades on my way to the living room to free him. He stretches his front legs out the crate door and brings out the toy he took to bed the night before. He shakes himself from nose to tail and stretches some more. I pat him on the head. The cats follow me from room to room until I make it to the kitchen.

Sometimes the cats eat first; other times it is the dog's turn. Regardless, I grab the dog food scoop and head to a closet where his plastic food container is stored. I tap my fingernails on the plastic scoop, and Speckles lies on the living room floor as flat as he can, waiting.

He won't eat his breakfast until he hears me rustle a plastic bag in the kitchen that contains small biscuits. I drop one on top of his food, wave my hand around the doorway, motioning him forward and he comes running. He looks up at me first and I kiss the top of his nose. He snatches the biscuit, takes it to the living room to eat it, and then he comes back to have breakfast. I fill his other bowl with cool water.

The cats stand in the kitchen waiting for their turn. Opening the cat food cupboard door, I select the top food can. Each week I stagger their entrees so they eat a different meal twice a day. Again, I tap my fingernails on the top of the aluminum can, and they start to meow and move to the sink. Desi uses a chair to climb to the countertop. C.D. gracefully flies up to the surface from the floor. I mention to them what the entrée is and they respond to *chicky chunks, beefy gravy* or *turkey giblets*.

One can, split in half, feeds both of them. They usually jockey for positions, one on either end of the sink, their backs to each other with their tails touching at the tip.

Once they are through eating, Speckles sniffs inside of the garbage can to see what his sisters ate for breakfast. Then he is escorted outside for his morning run.

Before I go to work, Speckles stands in the kitchen doorway waiting for a *big boney* to nibble on while I'm at work.

At night the feeding routine is similar, normally beginning at 5 p.m., followed by cleaning the litter box and sweeping up litter tracked across the kitchen floor. At the end of the day I pick up all the toys Speckles has scattered on the floor and on furniture and place them back in his toy box beside his crate.

When it is time for bed, I say *night-night* to Speckles, and he walks back to his crate, waiting for a biscuit and a toy to take to bed. Desi and C.D. follow

me to the bedroom and decide if they will sleep with
me.

Fascination

My neighbor has a yellow cat. I found out from the paperboy in our subdivision that the kitty's name is Nip and that he lives two doors north of me.

Since I just moved into my house last November, I started spotting Nip in the spring with his collar tags jingling from the collar around his neck. From the look in his eyes, the position of his tail high in the air, and his stride, I could tell he owned the subdivision I lived in.

Across the street from this cat's house and mine is a river. Every morning and every evening Nip makes his way to the water to snoop around. Speckles spots Nip through the picture window in our living room and whimpers until I come and watch what he's watching.

One afternoon, Nip was standing under a pine tree on the border of our property. I spotted him and decided to make friends with him. Speckles was watching us through the window, whining with frustration because I was befriending this feline he had watched for months.

It took a few minutes, but Nip came to me slowly. I sat in the grass and he approached my hand. He then flopped onto the ground and rolled over onto his back. We chatted for a while, and then he jogged across the yard to attend to his afternoon rounds.

It's funny, the little things that will fascinate an animal, rather like a human amused by watching people at a shopping mall.

This morning, my little orange friend was making his way to the river when a white butterfly distracted him. He sat and watched it wiggling in the air, then it landed on a blade of grass. Nip stalked the butterfly, keeping his belly low to the ground. Speckles and I watched from the picture window. When the butterfly flew upward, Nip sprang off of the ground and grabbed at the air, missing the butterfly. When Nip landed, he looked around and then went about his business as usual.

When he leaped into the air, Speckles bumped his nose against the picture window, trying to participate in the fun.

Speckles and my cats also find flying-insects fascinating. Several days ago, Speckles was walking beside the flower planters on our patio, sniffing the blooms, when suddenly a butterfly and a bumblebee came at him at once. He bit at the air, but the butterfly continued to flutter behind his head and the bumblebee zoomed back and forth in front of his nose. This kept him occupied for a short while.

Months ago, Speckles and I were in the yard together. I was gardening and Speckles started barking beside me. When I looked to see what had disturbed him, I noticed him pointing at my neighbor's wind catcher. This wind catcher is a man rowing a boat, and when the wind catches it, the oars spin round and round. The gizmo is attached to the top of a pole along our fence, and that day the gizmo squeaked as it rowed.

Speckles thought the thing was a bird. He barked sporadically at this ornament for at least half an hour. I tried to explain what it was, but he didn't believe me.

My cats like to catch maple tree seeds as they spin through the air like helicopter propellers. Each season when the seeds fall, the cats wait for me to find nice, plump ones to toss to them so they can flip through the air trying to catch them.

Large leaves from trees also keep Speckles occupied in the fall. They tumble over the grass and he chases them like they are squirrels.

Good-Byes and Hellos

Any time I leave my house, a face or three appear in the windows to watch me go.

Speckles places his feet in the dining room windowsill and stands tall on his hind legs. From the street, all I can see is his white chest, pink nose, and his floppy orange ear tips. He'll watch me walk down the sidewalk, get into my car, and drive out of sight. His head tilts and bobs to find a better view.

If he isn't looking out of the dining room window, he is standing by the front door, looking through the small panes of glass. Since it is older, rippled glass, he has to move his head around to see me clearly.

Most often, his tongue droops low while he examines my movements. Seldom does he whine or bark.

I wave to him, tell him goodbye and then climb into my car, waving again before I go. I often wonder what the neighbors think of my behavior.

When I do yard work, he follows me from window to window as I work my way around the house. In the back bedroom, he stands on a bed and puts his feet on the cat's window seat.

Speckles and Desi vie for the door and dining room window positions each time I leave. Desi can sit in the windowsill, but she has to stand on her hind feet to look out the front door window.

If I leave and she is in the window, the dog chases her away with his nose and she runs to the door. If she is by the door, he gooses her with his nose and she runs to the window.

Upstairs in our house is an arched, narrow window with a wide sill. My other cat, C.D., positions herself there and peers down at me. Since she is black and white, people usually only see her white blotches.

Desi is the talker in the house. She will tell me when she wants to run out the door and nibble on grass, when she wants to come inside and when she wants me to take her with me.

When she is behind the front door glass, I see her mouth open and close, talking to me.

When she is sitting in the screened window, I hear her from the street, meowing at me. If I say her name, she meows louder.

My parents, who live across the street from me, have heard her meowing at me on occasion. My mom sometimes stands on her front porch and yells, "Hello Desi Mo Mo!" and Desi responds with a high-pitched, "Meow!"

Desi comes from a long line of greeters and farewell givers. Her sister, who was adopted by an elderly couple when she was a kitten, sits in their window and waves goodbye to the couple when they go away. She puts her feet on the glass and paws up and down. They told me they enjoy waving back at her, and they have taken pictures of her doing this talented act.

It breaks my heart to see my pets' faces in the windows when I leave, but at the same time, it makes me feel good to know so many little lives depend on me and miss me when I am gone. Every time I come

home, I call their names, then hug and kiss each one
of them.

Open Door Policy

Since I live alone, well, with my pets, I have a habit of not closing my bathroom door while I'm in bathroom taking care of business.

I tried a few times to close the door behind me, but little paws instantly poke under the bottom crack of the door, persistently scratch on the door, claw at the carpet outside of the door or attempt to pull open the door from the bottom by grabbing it with claws.

For some reason, what I might be doing behind that closed door for a couple of minutes causes my pets separation anxiety. Therefore, I instilled an open-door policy between us.

Maybe they're so persistent because I seldom sit still for very long. When I'm in *down time*, my pets seek me out for affection no matter where I am.

The thing is, I have four cats and one sixty-pound dog and a bathroom barely big enough for one adult to turn around in. When they all pack the room with me, personalities start to conflict, paws sometimes start flying, and they'll often take swats at their brothers and sisters. The whole time, I'm pretty much confined to my porcelain throne in one corner, waiting for the conflict to end.

It's not uncommon at one time to find Joan sitting in the bathtub watching me, Desdemona sitting on a rug beside Speckles who is leaning against my legs,

Jack perched on the sink waiting for a drink of running water and C.D. examining us from the doorway, wondering how she can get closer to me without being stepped on or swatted in the face.

When I stand up, they all scurry out of the room, growling at each other, jumping over each other and so forth.

Several times I have just lightly pushed the door shut in an effort to keep warmth in the room while I showered. I inevitably find a little black-and-white nose poking through the door crack, and then a head emerges followed by a body. Then the door stands open a couple of feet again.

I find that this desire by my pets to see what I'm doing behind closed doors applies to just about every room in our home. They fear they might miss out on some stimulating activity and a pat on the head from their mom.

So you see, if I don't leave my bathroom door open once they all enter the room, it would be like tossing me into pool of piranhas. At least with an open door, we can all escape freely if conflict arises.

Pet Names

I have often found myself calling my pets by names other than ones I gave them. I guess you could call these names their *pet names*.

One day I listened to myself saying these names and wondered if other pet owners do the same thing with their pets. Maybe my habit stems from childhood when my mom used to call me many names, including "boo boo bear" and "pumpkin."

I decided to share with you some of the pet names I have given to my cats, Desdemona, C.D., Captain Jack Sparrow and Joan of Arc; and my dog, Speckles.

Desdemona is usually referred to in relaxed settings as Desi. When she is eating food from my plate or running out the front door unexpectedly, I use her real name, Desdemona. At other times, I call her:

Desdemona Lisa, Desolita, Mona Lisa, Desde Mona Lisa, Monie, Desi Mo Mo, Mo Mo, Boo, Boo Ghostie (because she is white), and Mona Lisa Conchita Conspita Alonzo.

I generally call C.D. by her real name, which is short for Chocolate Drop because of her white paws and black toes. Other times I call her:

C.D. Weedie, Deeter, C.D. Wheat Thin, Wheat Thin Cracker, Deeter Weeter and C.D.-La Quinta.

Speckles is the name I normally use for my

Brittany spaniel because he is constantly in trouble. On the rare occasions when he is calm, I call him:

Speck, Specktilius, Speckter, Speckalita, Speckmeister, Specktus, Speckaleena, MiMi, MiMi-lel-li, Mig, Tinkus and Tink Tink (because his nails make a *tink* noise on tile floors).

Captain Jack Sparrow was first named Sparrow. So I interchange the names Jack and Sparrow at random. For fun, I use these names:

Jackie, Jack-ita, Flap Jack, Lumber Jack, Hungry Jack, Jack-a-lope, Jack-ita and Sparrow-diferous,

I generally call Joan of Arc by that name, but I sometimes use the following:

Joanie, Joan-ita, Bird-ita, Birditicus, Bird-iferous, Jay Bird, Birdie, Joanie Baloney and Icky Tail.

Amazingly, my pets each answer to their pseudonyms. I think that they hear the vowel sounds most of all and then come running.

I have come to realize that if I ever have a child, it probably will never know its real name.

Saying "Good-bye" to Daddy

It has been nearly a year since my husband and I separated. Now we are divorced. He left one morning, saying he would be gone to another state for only three weeks on business. The truth is, he didn't intend to come back.

I became a single parent, or so to speak, of Speckles, Desdemona and C.D.

All of my furry children love me unconditionally. They spent most of their time with me prior to my divorce, while my husband was working long hours. The cats, ages six and seven, have been with me since they were born.

Desdemona didn't miss my husband very much, but C.D. remembered his distinct ear scratches in the evenings or afternoons when he would lie on the bed with her. He bonded with her, even though she was skittish around him at first. He scratched her ears by placing his hand on one side of her head and running his fingers from the middle of her head to the tip of her ear.

She melted when he did this. Her eyes squinted and her head leaned into his grip. I wondered if she was being tortured, but she kept coming back for more.

Since he left, I haven't been able to mimic this ear scratch and make her melt that way again.

Speckles is the one who misses his Daddy the most.

The day my husband left with most of his clothes, he kissed Speckles and told him, "Be good for Mommy." Speckles knew that something odd was happening. He ran from window to window, whining and watching Daddy pull his car out of the driveway.

I remember hugging Speckles and sitting on a window seat, telling him that Daddy would be back soon.

The story of my gradual separation from my husband is a long one, but before I knew he wasn't coming back, he would call occasionally and talk to Speckles over the phone. Speckles would turn his head to better hear Daddy's voice.

At first, each time Speckles jumped onto our bed, he would walk to the headboard and sniff cautiously around the pillows, trying to see if Daddy was there. He was used to visiting my husband while he took a nap, licking his face, and snuggling up under his chin with his head.

Since then, he has never been calm enough to lie with me like this. He visits me in bed, but only to nudge me with his wet, pink nose, sit still for a moment, and then crawl away.

My ex-husband now visits Speckles and me occasionally. I always tell Speckles, "Daddy's coming," and his ears lift a little higher.

Speckles immediately nuzzles up to his Daddy's side, licks his mouth and settles down a whole lot when my ex asks, "How's Daddy's boy?"

It breaks my heart every time my ex-husband

leaves. Each time he goes, he leaves Speckles waiting again.

When he goes, I think a piece of Speckles' heart goes with him. Speckles ceremoniously watches him, sitting on the window seat as Daddy backs his car out of the driveway.

He still goes back to the bedroom and sniffs the pillows, looking for Daddy.

Speckles senses when I feel alone. I hold him at night while sitting on the window seat, and we look up and down the road. I remember the days when Daddy would come home after work, no matter what time of the night.

Today, I am strong for myself and for my furry children. I will always be their mother, their protector, and unconditional friend.

Saying "Good-bye" To Pepper

My mom called me early one morning. She wanted me to meet her and my brother, Derek, at our veterinarian's office.

My brother had decided that it was time to put Pepper, his cat of fourteen years, to sleep.

Pepper had been suffering for several months from an enlarged heart. Gradually, fluid filled his chest cavity, making breathing difficult. Aside from this, his kidneys were failing. His weight had decreased, leaving him skin and bones covered by an unattractive coat of fur. Toward the end, he just slept in a living room chair, breathing heavily and eating *people food* (such as steak and roast) because that was all that enticed him.

My mom cut pieces of meat into tiny bites so Pepper could swallow them easily. Since his heart was enlarged and fluid pressed against his chest, his esophagus decreased in size, allowing only small morsels to pass through.

Every once in a while he would trick us by running through the house, climbing a tall scratching pole or jump across a chair to a window.

These bursts of energy made us believe that, with continued medication, he would live a couple more years. But he became more lifeless and was obviously unhappy. His eyes told us what he wanted. He didn't want to just lie in a chair, urinate countless times a day due to his medications and watch people and other pets passing him by.

He used to walk with us on a leash outside, climb the roof of my parents' house to monitor the neighborhood from above, rub all over my brother while he sat on the floor watching television, go to bed each night in an upstairs bathroom, and sit on my brother's lap, no matter where he rested.

The day before our trip to the vet, I saw Pepper at my parents' house. He was in his favorite reclining chair, and I knelt beside him, cradling his head in the palms of my hands.

"I love you," I whispered in his ear and kissed him. He purred and rested his head on the chair seat.

My mom held Pepper in a cat carrier when she and my brother entered the vet's office. Pepper's eyes were their usual golden spheres, but this time they spoke of fear and discomfort. He was panting when we pulled him gently out of the carrier. His lungs were unable to take in enough air, especially when he was nervous and afraid.

I held him over my shoulder and kissed him again, trying to hold back my tears.

Seeing a veterinary assistant waiting to take him away made me hold Pepper tighter. Derek patted him on the head, and my mom shed a few tears.

The assistant asked if my brother wanted to stay with Pepper while he was being euthanized. Derek said, "No."

Another assistant took Pepper from me and held him close. I still remember Pepper's eyes looking at me while the assistant took him away.

For fourteen years Pepper was a part of my life; that was half of my lifetime. In just a moment, we said goodbye.

I cried, grabbing tissues on the counter.

We still miss Pepper's deep meow when he stood by my parent's back door, begging to go outside. We miss him running through the house, over end tables and up the scratching pole.

We just miss him.

These memories of him as healthy and happy are good ones. He is happy now too, and I believe he understood our decision to end his suffering.

Sleeping Positions

I had a roommate in college who slept in a frog-like position. She'd lie on her stomach, arms bent at the elbow above her head and her legs spread wide with her knees pulled up toward her sides.

That was the first time I took notice of odd human sleeping positions. Now I take note of my pets' peculiar sleeping positions.

There's Speckles, who loves to lie on his stomach in a frog-like position, his back legs spread wide with inner thighs flat on the floor and his front paws extended out, usually holding a rawhide bone.

There is C.D., who, when she feels safe from the dog pouncing on her, lies on her back with all four legs in the air and her feet curled over.

Desdemona likes to stretch and contort her long body as far as she can reach. One day I found her partially upside down, with her lower body twisted one way and her upper body the other way. Her legs were stretched above her head and she pulled her body tight like a rubber band.

My mom's cat, Callie, can be spotted frequently bunched up in a praying Buddha-like position. She lays her forehead flat on the floor or scratching post platform and wraps her paws up around her head. A box of dishes could fall beside her and she wouldn't budge.

My mom's other cat, Spike, likes to lie on his tummy with his front legs stretched out long in front of him and his paws lying delicately on top of one another. This I call the *praying position.*

Whether it's a cat curled up in a shoe box or a dog flat on his side in the middle of the kitchen floor, watching an animal sleep is relaxing to the heart and soul.

I enjoy when my cats sleep with me at night. Desdemona lies strategically between my feet. She knows I will shift my legs around her body throughout the night instead of flicking her onto the floor unexpectedly.

C.D. has taken a liking to my pillow when I am sleeping. I wake up lying on the mattress and she's taken over my pillow.

While it is relaxing to watch pets sleep, I love to sneak up and play tricks on them, just like they do to me when I am busy or sleeping.

My favorite animal part is an exposed pink belly. I crawl along the floor on my hands and knees and give them an unexpected zerbert on their belly with my lips. The noise and feel makes them spring to their feet.

Desdemona gets me back in the mornings when my alarm clock goes off and I do not move out of bed. She rises from her spot between my feet, walks up my torso, stepping hard on my full bladder, and sits on my chest, staring me in the face. She looks around for my fingers and chews delicately on each one until I pet her or get up and feed her.

C.D. likes to stand beside me while I sleep, working her claws in the bed covers. Her ammunition is drool, which she produces when she is content. She aims the stream over my face and shakes her head to-and-fro, dispersing it like a showerhead.

Socialization of Pets and People

One afternoon I was watering flowers in the backyard and walked out front to find Speckles playing with two neighborhood children. His pink tongue was dangling, his ears were perked up, and the kids were patting their chests, trying to get him to jump up on them. When he did, they ran the other way.

Speckles was at the end of his rope – so to speak. His tie-out stake and red cord prevented him from following the children home, which I am sure he would have loved to do.

His tennis ball became the next object of play. The boy would throw the ball to the girl, and Speckles would run after it as it soared through the air. Each child stood far enough away from the end of Speckles' cord so that when the ball came, he couldn't get it. He flipped himself several times when the cord drew tight. Then he learned his boundaries and stopped running before he choked himself.

The kids laughed at him, and he enjoyed their attention.

I stepped aside into a flowerbed in front of the house and continued to watch him. He'd look at me occasionally, wondering why I didn't help him.

Pets are like children. I hear Speckles bark and I

run to see what is wrong. If he appears sick, I hold him, rub his warm head, and sing to him. If he grabs something to chew that could hurt him, I stick my fingers into his mouth to get it out.

That afternoon when the kids were harmlessly tormenting him, I had to stay nearby to watch my baby. Every once in a while I would say "Oh, poor Speckles," "Get em', Speckles," "Almost got it, Speckles" and "Good boy!"

I started to realize that I had seen the children somewhere before, so I went closer to talk to them. They said they owned Buck, a yellow Labrador Speckles' age that lives nearby.

Speckles pulls me in Buck's direction every time he takes me for a walk. They rub noses through a chain-link fence, grunting doggy talk with hind-ends wiggling.

The kids had seen us there many times and ran out occasionally to see Speckles.

Once, Buck got loose and headed south to our house. He darted across the front yard and Speckles smelled him through the window screen. A lot of snorting and barking took place before my husband cornered Buck outside and took him home.

Dogs make friends, just as children and adults do. They know who will bite and growl at them. They know who will stop, shift back and forth like a football player, and run in circles until they wear themselves out with delight.

Just as adults visit friends and family for socialization, so should pets. Even Desdemona comes running when she hears a foreign voice in the house. She rolls on the floor and rubs all over a visitor enjoying their "Ooohs" and "Aaahs."

For your sake, and your dog's, schedule daily walks so they can meet other pooches, and you can meet other people in the neighborhood. Invite people over so they can meet your cat or whatever pets you have.

The Words They Know

Within one hour after I gave Speckles a new stuffed animal, he knew its name.

I purchased a short, white duck at a garage sale fund-raiser for a local animal foundation. At home, I washed it and fluffed it dry. He immediately took it in his mouth and shook it. Then he tossed it in the air and caught it. When he was tired, he laid his head on it, and when we left him home alone, he took it into his crate.

When that fuzzy duck disappears, all I have to say to him is, "Go get your duckie!" He starts sniffing the house until he finds it.

Both cats and dogs are intelligent. I am a firm believer in that. They may not be able to do mathematical problems or bake a cake (though that would be nice to come home to), but they can identify words with objects and actions.

Speckles knows several commands and words. Among them are: get your bony, go home (meaning his crate), want your brekus? (short for breakfast), din din (short for dinner), hungy? (short for hungry), treat (time for a little biscuit), cube (meaning ice cube), drinky (usually a drink out of the bathtub faucet or garden hose), inside (what I say to bring him into the house), truckie (he would dash from the house into my husband's pickup truck for a ride), sit, stay, down, no bite (when he playfully gnaws on my fingers), drop it (when he grabs plastic cups, shampoo bottles and other items he shouldn't have) and, of course – No!

My cats, C.D. and Desdemona have a great deal of intelligence, too. They both know words including: din din (along with a fingernail tap on their food dishes), brekus, up (to come up on the bed, sofa or table), outside (to go outside and roll on the sidewalk), chicky (short for chicken), beefy (short for beef dinner), paper wad (their game before bedtime) and No! (needed when they are stealing a chicken leg off my plate or eating my ferns).

I have a certain eye-contact communication with my cats, too. We look at each other, and their pupils widen and follow me throughout a room. I can wave my hand or fingers in a *Come* type of motion and they jump up and follow me.

I am offended if anyone calls my furry children stupid or funny looking. My husband repeatedly tells me that my pets don't understand the difference between "You beautiful little hairy goddess", and "You ugly, fat weasel." I tell him, "Don't say that to her. You will hurt her feelings." He shakes his head in disbelief.

I read somewhere that animals identify with sounds in words. Like the name C.D., in which C.D. probably hears the "e" sounds. I also think that they can tell by the tone of your voice when you call them nice names versus bad ones.

My mom's dog, Sugar, cowers when anyone tells her, "Bad dog, Sugar!" If she eats cat food, my mom says those three words, and Sugar runs away and curls up on the sofa or in her bed. My husband liked to randomly torture Sugar with those words.

One evening while we were sitting in my parents' living room and Sugar was asleep on the floor with all four legs in the air, my husband decided to say, "Bad dog, Sugar!" This made her shake and immediately curl up on the sofa. She eyed the room' trying to figure out what she did wrong.

Animals, like humans, understand physical and verbal abuse. Most dogs know the difference between garbage scraps and a good bowl of healthy dog food. They appreciate the softness of a sofa over a hard dirt floor. They smile a tongue-lolling smile when they receive ice cubes on a hot day.

Cats appreciate curling up under a thermal blanket versus sleeping under a bush outside. They'd rather eat fresh shrimp than pluck feathers from a dead sparrow.

We are our pets' parents. We are responsible for teaching them. The more time we spend educating them, the more they will know.

Wake Up Calls

My friend, Jo, used to tell me stories about her black-and-white male cat named J.R. Every morning he would sit close to her head while she was sleeping and sneeze precisely into her face. She said it was his way of telling her it was time to get up.

I have my own set of four-legged alarm clocks that, without fail, take turns waking me each morning when the sun peeks over the horizon. Each has their own unique method of making me rise.

Desdemona stands on the kitchen sink and meows at me from a distance, hoping I will stagger in to feed her. If I don't respond to her calls instantly, she'll make her way to my bed, stand beside the head-end of the bed and meow at me.

I sometimes dangle my arm over the side of the mattress and pet her on the head, telling her to *hold on* or *be quiet*. She proceeds to nibble delicately on each of my fingertips until I get up to feed her.

C.D has her own subtle tactics to get me moving. There's nothing more irritating than whiskers tickling your face while you sleep. That's what C.D. does, lying on my pillow and placing her face directly in front of mine. Time and time again I wake to find her looking me in the eyes.

Joan of Arc has a rougher way of waking me. She scurries up the bed beside me, head-butts my face with her wet nose, and sticks her nose in my ear. If I do not start to move, she begins licking my face just along the hairline. If she sees my eyes move, she licks my tender eyelids with her harsh, sandpaper-like tongue.

When Speckles hears me moving slightly in the morning, he begins to jump around with anticipation of his morning potty break. He will stand beside the bed, stare up at me and then walk out of the room. This repeats several times with intermittent moaning. If he doesn't get a response, he leaps onto the bed for several seconds and then back down to the floor. He does this repeatedly. As a last resort, he sniffs my face with his large wet nose.

Jack Sparrow is my newest alarm clock, and he has a unique method that initially startled me, but now makes me laugh.

One morning before my alarm went off, Jack jumped up on my bed and sat motionless for a bit. I can always feel him when he lands on the mattress because he weighs a hefty sixteen pounds.

I started dozing off again when suddenly Jack had a chunk of my hair in his mouth, grasping it at my scalp and pulling with all his might. He startled me and I startled him when I moaned, "Hey – What are you doing?"

I thought this behavior would end that morning, but since then he's pulled my hair often in the early morning hours. Even though it still startles me, I just say his name and he lies down on the bed beside me.

Pets truly do help keep us active, and these early morning rituals are just part of their strategy.

In Closing

Speckles

Just before Speckles turned twelve, he started to have trouble breathing. At first, I thought he had an allergy issue. He always had seasonal allergies, mostly sneezing.

I took him to a veterinarian and initially he took Benadryl to ease sneezing and stuffy nose symptoms. Still, he continued to concern me with labored breathing that came and went.

One day a veterinarian told me that Speckles' breathing problem sounded as though it was resonating from his throat – i.e., his larynx. She suggested I take him for an advanced exam at the Veterinary Teaching Hospital at the University of Illinois in Urbana, Ill.

Speckles' bark had also begun to sound hoarse, which validated this veterinarian's words.

During an overnight stay at the U of I, I was told Speckles would need to be sedated for a scope of his larynx and lungs. Because of his labored breathing, there was a risk that he could die during the exam. I had my first dose of reality as I signed paperwork agreeing to give the veterinary clinic permission to do the exam, and that I accepted the risks. I knew that my baby boy needed to be diagnosed and treated.

I left Speckles at the clinic overnight and he kept his big stuffed moose with him for comfort.

Veterinary students called me with updates on his health while he was there. For that, I am eternally grateful.

I was saddened to learn that Speckles had two serious health issues: a paralyzed larynx and partially collapsed lungs (the lower portion of both of them). Why he developed these conditions we will never know. I was told that it sometimes happens in older dogs.

He could have undergone costly surgery to open his larynx a bit more so he could get air through it less stressfully. However, the surgery would have been hard on him because of his labored breathing. The surgery could have also taken his life.

His partially collapsed lungs could not be helped.

I asked a veterinarian at the U of I what he would do if this were his dog. He told me what I already felt in my heart – just keep Speckles comfortable for the remainder of his life. I also asked the veterinarian what symptoms I should look for that meant Speckles was suffering and needed to be euthanized. We discussed those symptoms. The main one was labored breathing that lasted a long time.

Speckles came home with me, along with medication for him to take twice a day that would help airways in his lungs expand a little better.

I also tried to keep him as calm as possible – which was not easy, him being a Brittany. His joy of running after squirrels and playing with stuffed animals overcame him.

There were a few times I had to force him to stay still until he could breathe easier. Once he lay down in ornamental grasses just off of my patio, and I had to pick him up and carry him back to the house.

I also told my local veterinarians, who had an office just a few blocks away from my home, that I might need to rush Speckles to their clinic sometime for oxygen.

I told my family and friends about Speckles' diagnosis and that I had promised Speckles I would be there for him as long as we were blessed to be together.

Three months after that veterinary visit at the U of I, the aforementioned *symptoms* appeared.

The following letter I sent by e-mail and snail mail to friends and neighbors the day after Thanksgiving, 2007.

"Hello.

I sent this message to many people by email Thanksgiving night. I wanted to share with you, too, since you knew my dog Speckles.

After Thanksgiving dinner with my family, I came home to Speckles, and we shared some pumpkin pie and Cool Whip together. Shortly after that, around 7 p.m., he went into serious breathing distress.

Earlier this summer at the U of I Vet Clinic, Urbana, he was diagnosed with collapsed lungs (only his main airways were open) and a paralyzed larynx. I was told he could live months or years, depending on his age and how well I kept him calm, and taking oral meds two times daily to keep his lungs dilated a bit more than normal. He turned 12 on September 21. I've had him since he was 3 months old.

He was doing well on medication, but the last two weeks he often seemed to be in greater distress.

Last night after his breathing distress started, he

lost control of his bodily functions and I called an emergency vet in Mokena – 45 miles from my house – the only veterinary ER clinic close.

They said he needed oxygen, or he would die. They said I could chance leaving him at home and let him calm down and, hopefully he would come out of it, or he might not.

He was not getting better.

I drove at illegal speeds to Mokena – holding him with one hand behind me – he threw up and pottied in the car and was lying on the seat with seriously labored breathing.

When I got to the clinic, he walked into the clinic, and a doctor carried him to a room and put him on a ventilator.

They sedated him, too.

When I saw Speckles, he had oxygen running to his lungs directly and he was sleeping – sedated.

I talked with the doctor – an X-ray also showed some fluid in Speckles' lungs.

The doctor told me that Speckles' troubles would probably worsen now. I asked him his honest opinion – would Speckles suffer more now and if so, would the vet choose to put him to sleep if he was in my shoes.

He said he would probably "let him go."

So Speckles went to heaven at around 9 p.m. Thanksgiving night.

My heart cries for Speckles. And it will for some time. He was my son, an inspiration and a joy. We have been through so much together. He would always look out my front picture window while sitting on a cedar chest. This was his favorite place to watch for me. And my cats miss him. All loved him. And it seemed every stray dog around would end up at my house because Speckles was so friendly to everyone. I miss him painfully.

I spoke directly into his ear while he was sedated on the exam table – I hope he heard me. I told him I loved him and would see him again someday. I was crying, and my tears fell onto his face, beside his eye. I kissed him and lay over him for a short time as he was euthanized.

Thank you for loving him, too."

I still cry when I think about that night. I was alone when all of this happened. I drove home from the emergency veterinary office alone.

I came home to my cats, all of which were nervous about the activity they witnessed between Speckles and me when I tried to get him into my car and rush him to the clinic.

The next day, I had to clean the inside of my car. Speckles had pottied and thrown up several times on the way to the emergency clinic. While scrubbing the upholstery, I cried helplessly. He was gone, and all that I had left of him from that night was this. Even the sight of his remaining hairs on the car seats made me cry.

I shared with friends, neighbors, and family that I had lost my buddy. My neighbors saw me outside and came to hug me. I received at least fifteen sympathy cards from friends. Speckles was loved by so many people – tremendously. He will never be forgotten.

I remember much about the night Speckles died, but one thing stands out most of all. When the veterinarian at the emergency clinic picked Speckles up in the waiting room to carry him back to an exam room and place him on oxygen, Speckles struggled to stay with me – his mom. I remember telling the vet to *be careful* while Speckles continued to watch me, looking back to me as the doctor carried him away.

In his time of struggle, his time of pain, Speckles was still looking out for me.

The veterinarian at that clinic sent me a sympathy card soon after Speckles died. He met Speckles that one time, in a time of struggle, and this was the impression Speckles left on him:

"Although I knew Speckles very briefly, and not in health, he impressed me as a sweet dog with a gentle demeanor. Speckles was lucky to have had a good home where he was loved."

Desdemona

Desdemona was always a healthy girl. She was chunky, her fur was soft and shiny, and her eyes were bright and clean.

When she was about fifteen years old, I noticed a spot at the bottom of one of her eyes – on the iris, or colored portion of her eye. At first I thought it might be a freckle of some sort. But then, it started to grow and its edges appeared jagged.

My veterinarian said the spot was a tumor. Often, my veterinarian said, tumors in the eye were a sign of cancer somewhere else in the body – often in the abdomen or chest area.

Desdemona's blood tests were negative. She seemed healthy and happy. We could have removed her eye, but at her age, it would have been a traumatic operation for her. Also, if there was cancer elsewhere in her body, what good would it do to remove her eye?

I chose to monitor the growth of the eye tumor.

Shortly before her sixteenth birthday, Desi started to sound like she was moaning when she breathed – as if she had asthma and her airways were constricted. She had allergies from time to time, so asthma was a possibility.

I took her to the doctor for an exam. One way to detect asthma is to have a chest X-ray done. The X-ray will show white, circular patterns in the lungs.

When the veterinarian tacked the X-ray to a light box and showed me the results, we saw the circular patterns indicative of asthma. But what stood out, and the doctor emphasized to me, was a large mass in the middle of Desi's chest.

"It's a tumor," the veterinarian told me. It was not in her lungs or on her heart, but it was in her chest and was the size of a couple of golf balls put together.

Never did Desi show signs of distress. However, the moaning when she breathed was probably a sign. Now I knew that her eye tumor was a signal of a tumor in her chest.

After a long talk with the doctor, we agreed to give Desi medication to help her overcome her asthma and just let her live a happy life. Due to her age, I was not going to traumatize her with surgeries and cancer treatment.

On June 15, 2006, just two months after her sixteenth birthday, I woke in the early morning hours to hear Desi meowing from the kitchen. She often did this to make me feed her. I went into the kitchen and fed her and then headed back to bed.

Several minutes later, I heard her throwing up and then heard a meow I had never heard before and will never forget. It was a cry of pain, and I ran to her.

She was on the dining room floor, flat on her stomach and unable to breathe. I touched her and she fell onto her side, gasping gently for air.

I called an emergency veterinary clinic. The only emergency clinic near my home is forty-five minutes away. It was just before 4 a.m.

I explained to the doctor what had happened, about her history, and that I knew she was going to die if I couldn't get her oxygen. She was gasping for breath and unable to move.

The veterinarian told me, based on her immediate condition and her history of a chest tumor, something had apparently ruptured inside her. Rushing her to the doctor was an option, the doctor said, but she would probably die on the trip there.

I still remember the veterinarian telling me, "The best thing you can do for her right now is to hold her and let her go."

So I did.

She and I spent one hour together: me bending over her, holding her under a warm blanket, watching her die. I felt helpless. She was struggling, and I could do nothing to save her. Her whole life, from the day she was born under my desk in college, I was her friend and parent. She came to me for protection and love.

My other pets gathered around us in the dining room. They knew she was dying. They were quiet and rested near us.

I remember crying onto her face. I held her front paws in the palm of my right hand and she contracted them slowly, gently. I spoke into her ear that I loved her and I would see her again someday.

"The Lord is My Shepherd" came to mind and I recited it to her as she died. "Though I walk through the valley of the shadow of death, I fear no evil; for You are with me; Your rod and Your staff, they comfort me…."

I hoped it gave her peace. And as silly as it might sound, I baptized her, wiping a fingertip wet with my saliva on her forehead.

I had recently read a book, "Spirit Animals and the

Wheel of Life," by Hal Zina Bennett. In it, Bennett speaks of the Zuni culture of New Mexico. When the men of the tribe hunted, they would rush to a dying animal, press their lips to the mouth of that animal and exchange its last breaths with it. "This ritual," the book states, "is one of literally intermingling the spirits of the hunter and the hunted, of honoring the sacrifice and acknowledging their spiritual bonds."

I was bending over Desdemona that morning, my face close to hers, kissing her, and talking softly into her ear. I exchanged breaths with her. In those final moments, our spirits intermingled.

At 7 a.m., when our veterinarian's office opened, my mom came to help me. She drove me to the doctor's office as I held Desi's lifeless body in a blanket.

Chocolate Drop

C.D. lived her whole life having at least one grand mal seizure a year. In her senior years, the seizures came more frequently.

In the last few months of her life, C.D. started taking anti-seizure medication, which was recommended by her veterinarian. Her seizures had increased to roughly one per month. She also had thyroid issues and lost weight, reducing her to around five pounds.

C.D. loved to go outside in the garden with me. As tiny as she was, she still ran across the yard and climbed trees. Her favorite relaxation time was lying in the grass, flat on her side, in the sun. She was so thin. She looked like a black-and-white wafer.

Over the years, I'd learned that certain noises and sudden movements could trigger her seizures, such as my alarm clock going off in the morning, if I was typing fast at my computer and she was sitting beside it, or something in the house startling her.

The day Desdemona passed away on my dining room floor, my other pets, including C.D., gathered around us to observe and pay their respects.

A month after Desdemona died, C.D., age seventeen, suffered a grand mal seizure.

I had scheduled a veterinary appointment for Joan on July 31. She just needed routine vaccinations.

Joanie decided to fuss quite a bit over the trip and refused to go into a crate. The excitement of her fussing made C.D. go into a seizure.

That afternoon I took C.D. to the vet instead of Joan. I was so concerned about her. I thought she might need to be euthanized.

The vet drew some of C.D.'s blood that day and said it looked thin – like she was also anemic. Her heart rate was two hundred forty while the normal was one hundred forty.

I brought C.D. home and watched her carefully. That night she seemed to be in a daze. She drank a lot of water when she wasn't sleeping. She vomited and had diarrhea. She also meowed several times during the night.

For the last couple years of her life, she appeared to walk tenderly at times, as if she struggled with arthritis. The seizures, I'm sure, made her body hurt worse.

I think the stress of seeing her sister die contributed to the last major attack. This seizure, she simply could not come out of with strength.

That night, I comforted her, keeping her warm under a blanket and bringing her food and water. Still, C.D. had no ambition to walk. Her routine after-seizure behavior of strolling around the house to reacquaint herself with her surroundings did not happen.

Her eyes seemed drowsy and the pupils were large.

I remember resting on my knees in front of her as she lay on the floor. I kissed her and asked her softly, "What do you want me to do Deeter? Do you want to go to heaven? You let me know. I'll be with you."

I said a few prayers while petting her.

The next day, August 1, 2006, C.D. was still stationary, and she purred when I carried her to the veterinary office wrapped in a fleece blanket.

I held her while she was euthanized, kissed her head, and she purred until her last breath. I believe in my heart that she knew I was there, and she was ready to go. She knew she was leaving to go to a better life, without the crippling seizures and arthritis she endured in her senior years.

During her last few months, she enjoyed going outside in my fenced in yard, lying in the grass in the sun or shade and sleeping for hours. I watched her out a window to make sure she was safe. She was in her own little piece of heaven. I let her do whatever she desired.

I still have a framed picture of her when she was lying flat in the grass in the backyard, sunning her tiny body. In that photo, she has a peaceful smile on her face. That's how I remember my little "D."

Furry Faces I Have Known:
An Art Tribute

Annie

Baby

Bo

Bosley

Bruiser

Buddy

Callie

Chase

Daisy

Elizabeth

Ellie

Fat Boy

Goldie

Guinea Pig

Hope

Jake

Lil Buddy

Lily

Lincoln Logsdon

Louie

Mittens

Muffin

Pepper

Pet Rat

Pooper – 3 Weeks

Pooper – 3 Months

Pooper – 6 Months

Pooter

Princess

Puffy

Ruffy

Shadow

Skeeter

Smokey

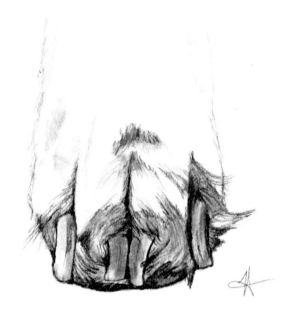

Speckle

Spike

Sweet Pea

Trixie

Tug

American Brittany Rescue

In honor of my Brittany spaniel, Speckles, a portion of the proceeds from this book will go to American Brittany Rescue.

American Brittany Rescue was formed in 1991 as a cooperative effort of Brittany owners, breeders, trainers, and fanciers who believed they have a responsibility not only for their own dogs and the dogs they produce, but also for the breed as a whole.

Because many rescue dogs can be traced one to three generations back to a recognized breeder, American Brittany Rescue believes that all breeders should take it upon themselves to assist Brittanies in need, in any way they can.

The purpose of American Brittany Rescue is to take in stray, abandoned, surrendered and/or impounded purebred Brittanies, provide them with foster care, health and temperament screening, offer an opportunity for rehabilitation if necessary, assure their health and place them in new homes.

Initially, American Brittany Rescue began with about eight volunteers nationwide. In 2009, the organization noted nine hundred seven volunteers in forty-nine states and in Canada.

In the beginning, all volunteers had to pay the

expenses for dogs in foster care and be reimbursed from the dog's adoption donation. Today, ABR works hard to find ways to help take the financial burden of fostering away from foster families.

Years ago, volunteers had to find adopters for dogs on their own.

With the creation of the American Brittany Web site, www.americanbrittanyrescue.org, networking to find new homes for Brittanies became more efficient.

Volunteers now have a swift way to advertise their foster dogs and screen applicants.

Each year, American Brittany Rescue takes in about one thousand Brittanies.

Over the years, American Brittany Rescue has added elements that enhance their rescue mission, including: Brittany Express that helps transport dogs from where they are (when there is no one available to foster them) to safety in another state, a Senior Companion Program, a Buddy Program, an Extended Family Tree and a Senior Retreat.

Brittanies make wonderful family dogs and excel in many areas, but they are not for everyone. They are loving, active, playful, energetic dogs that require personal attention every day. If you'd like to learn if a Brittany is a good choice for you, your family and/or your lifestyle, please see the American Brittany Rescue Website, www.americanbrittanyrescue.org.

You can also contact American Brittany Rescue at 1-866-BRIT911.

American Humane Association

The author has chosen to also donate a portion of this book's proceeds to the American Humane Association.

In the late 1800s, several Societies for the Prevention of Cruelty to Animals existed throughout the United States. Because of a publicized story about Mary Ellen Wilson of New York in 1873, the first Society for the Prevention of Cruelty to Children was created. This story revealed that Mary Ellen, age eight, had been severely abused by her stepparents.

Although these organizations were successful, they lacked a unified voice in promoting the humane movement. In 1877, delegates with twenty-seven humane organizations from ten states joined forces to combine their strengths and unite their missions. At this meeting the American Humane Association was founded.

Immediately the AHA addressed its first task, to put an end to the inhumane treatment of farm animals and deplorable conditions they were living in.

Since that meeting in 1877, the AHA has held true to its mission, to create a more humane and compassionate world by ending abuse and neglect of children and animals. The non-profit organization leads the way in understanding human-animal interaction and its role in society.

Every day the AHA reaches millions of people through groundbreaking research, education, training, and services that span a wide network of organizations, agencies, and businesses. Some ways the AHA is making a difference include:

● Starting Be Kind to Animals Week nearly one hundred years ago.

● Creating the "No Animals Were Harmed" program, the film and television industry's officially sanctioned on-set monitoring program for animal actors.

● Developing innovations to prevent child abuse, strengthen families and enhance child protection systems worldwide.

● Supporting the nation's animal shelters and rescue organizations, providing training and financial support to save animals, increase adoptions and serve their communities.

● Creating Adopt-A-Dog Month and Adopt-A-Cat Month to raise awareness and promote adoption of homeless pets.

● Forming a Red Star Animal Emergency Services team that is mobilized by states, counties and municipalities to rescue pets and other animals from disaster areas.

● Implementing the label American Humane Certified, the world's largest and fastest-growing humane farming consumer label.

● Using Action Alerts to inform supporters about legislation that could improve safety and wellbeing for children and animals.

For more information call the American Humane

Association, at 800-227-4645, go to their Website at
www.americanhumane.org,   or   e-mail   them   at
info@americanhumane.org

About the Author

It all began with writing a diary of short essays for Tracy Ahrens' own benefit in order to remember situations she experienced with her first three pets: Speckles, a Brittany spaniel; and cats, C.D. and Desdemona.

Through her volunteer work with different humane organizations, she realized that these stories could help other pet owners develop bonds with their pets like she has and make others laugh and learn about raising their furry children.

The diary of essays grew and became *Raising My Furry Children.* – highlighting the fact that for most pet owners, these creatures are like their children. Today, descriptions of *furry children* and being a *pet parent* are noted in books, magazines, and newspapers across the country.

If you'd like to contact Tracy Ahrens, please e-mail her at <u>mylittleforie@yahoo.com</u>

CPSIA information can be obtained at www.ICGtesting.com
Printed in the USA
BVOW021817151211

278487BV00008B/35/P